Every *Day* Was *Special*

Every Day Was Special

A Fly Fisher's Lifelong Passion

William G. Tapply

Foreword by Nick Lyons

Skyhorse Publishing

Skyhorse Publishing books may be purchased in bulk at special discounts for
sales promotion, corporate gifts, fund-raising, or educational purposes. Special
editions can also be created to specifications. For details, contact the Special
Sales Department, Skyhorse Publishing, 555 Eighth Avenue, Suite 903, New
York, NY 10018 or info@skyhorsepublishing.com.

www.skyhorsepublishing.com

10 9 8 7 6 5 4 3 2 1

Library of Congress Cataloging-in-Publication Data

Tapply, William G.
Every day was special : a fly fisher's lifelong passion /
     William G. Tapply.
p. cm.
ISBN 978-1-60239-955-6 (alk. paper)
1. Fly fishing—Anecdotes. 2. Tapply, William G. 3. Fishers—
     United States--Biography. I. Title.
SH456.T349 1997
799.12'4—dc22
2009045558

Printed in the United States of America

Contents

Foreword

Every Day Was Special registers much of the measure of a special human being. Bill Tapply is always present in these reports of days on the water—always curious, with great common sense, down-home warmth, passion, unflagging good cheer and wit, a generous spirit, a flair for adventure, and a positive genius for friendship. You cannot help but love the man. You learn with and from him, enjoy fishing (in print) with him, share his lifelong joy in all manner of fishing (especially with a fly) and feel everywhere a balance and modesty rare among folk who write about this sport. If style is the man—and I think it surely is—Bill gives us, in every word he wrote, a man who truly could find every day on the water to be special.

Bill died of leukemia at age sixty-nine in late July 2009, after a two-year struggle with the disease; during this time, he wrote at least five books. He had taught high school for twenty-five years in Lexington, Massachusetts, and then, when he began to publish his first novels, at Emerson College and as writer-in-residence at Clark University. He wrote more than twenty excellent mystery novels featuring a fly-fishing detective named Brady Coyne, of whom he explained: "He has neither the cynical world view of some private eyes nor the excessive honor of others. . . . he's very much like me. I'd rather have you identify with him than admire him. He's not bigger than life. He's just about life-sized." He wrote other mysteries, too, and a fine book about how to write the stuff; and he also wrote numerous articles about fly fishing and upland-bird hunting for *Field & Stream, Sports Illustrated, American Angler,* and others, and a dozen books on those subjects, most of which I was proud to edit or publish. He had been an excellent athlete in high school and remained so well into his adult years. Bill was a quiet, kind man who knew how to listen and was adept at the fishing and bird-hunting he loved. Everyone who knew him or read what he wrote will miss this patient, thoughtful man.

What we have and never need miss, of course, are his words. *Every Day Was Special*—finished not long before he died and due off press in the spring, a time he loved for its augury of yet another new season—has some of his best words. It is a full and consistently engaging collection that traces the arc of his fishing life from his first days fishing in a nearby pond to days on western spring creeks, on ocean flats and warmwater lakes, and practical advice on a whole range of matters piscatorial. Of those first days, and of the "hook" that led him to a lifetime of sport, he writes: "It's been a lifelong, ever-expanding journey, with many big fish and faraway waters and dramatic moments . . . and yet I don't think any of those moments or any of those places or fish has thrilled me any more than seeing the twitch of my fly line where it entered the muddy waters of my backyard pond . . ."

Though he fished and hunted birds with the likes of his father— the great "Tap" Tapply—Lee Wulff, Frank Woolner, Ollie Rodman, Burt Spiller, and others of their ilk—his early days are characterized most by what he learned by himself. His father encouraged him to find his own sport and he did, and what he reports in this book are the first-hand observations of a man who experienced it all himself and never stopped learning. There is a happy and irresistible freshness and New England independence to his thoughts. I especially like the way he explores some of the more controversial issues, such as whether a particular brand of fishing is somehow "better" or "higher" than another. He even-handedly explains that though he eschews snobbishness about the methods of pursuit one chooses, he happens to love beyond all else the dramatic rise of a trout to a dry fly. He never knocks another man's sport and only repeats what his father rightly notes, that a man can be as much of a hog whether he fished with a worm or a fly. I like too that he can change his mind. In the remarkable tailwater fishing now available throughout the country, he has found ample good reason not to despise the Army Corps of Engineers, for their dam building, as his father did and he did for decades, as I blindly did for many years before fishing below dams in Arkansas, Montana, and New York State.

Bill loved the quiet rituals of angling: being with friends he held close—Andy, Marshall, Norm, and others—at given times, and the rhythmic return to such places with such people year after year. He had special passions, like fishing the challenging spring creeks of the West, and the subtleties of fly fishing, like discovering how best to fish when the trout are taking ants or midges, perhaps. He loved challenging days fishing in salt water, for blues, bonefish, redfish, snook, or stripers, and all his life he was devoted to bass-bug fishing, begun with his father for smallmouth on New Hampshire lakes and enduring until his last summer. He wrote wonderfully well about bass-bugging—both in a solid practical book and numerous essays; less than a year ago, when his cancer was in remission, he made me swear that we would fish for largemouth bass together this past August, that he'd bring plenty of bugs and would trailer his rowboat to my corner of the Catskills and row me around. It did not happen.

Bill was also a devoted and careful fly tier, and this book ends with solid advice on how to tie some extremely effective patterns for bass, trout, saltwater fish, and his favorite New England flies. Like his father's great bass bug, which Bill tied to perfection, his approach to all fly tying—and all fishing (and in fact all of his life and all of his writing) was simple, elegant, practical, and wise. *Every Day Was Special* is filled with these qualities, in its deceptively easy prose, entertaining anecdotes, and sensible suggestions that cannot help but improve the quality and success of a reader's fly-fishing life.

The fine mystery writer Vicki Stiefel, his longtime companion and wife, said that Bill was her soul mate, her joy, her best friend—a very special person with whom she shared an interesting and compelling life. Letting his many friends know that he was gone, she wrote: "My beloved Bill died last night. His passing was soft, and he was surrounded by myself and his five children. He will be missed."

You bet he will.

—**Nick Lyons**
December 2009

Every *Day* Was *Special*

Introduction

Just as the twig is bent, the tree's inclined.

—Alexander Pope, *Moral Essays*

When I was a kid growing up in the suburbs, a warm-water pond lay just over the hill and through the woods behind my house. In the endless summer days of my boyhood, armed with a hand-me-down bamboo fly rod (a mass-produced South Bend 8-footer with a shortened tip), an old Pfleuger reel wound with a cracked HDH double-taper line, an envelope of size-6 Eagle Claw bait hooks, a spool of 8-pound monofilament, and a Campbell's soup can of freshly dug earthworms, I haunted the place. I learned how to handle a fly rod by rollcasting a hook impaled with a gob of worms (you couldn't make an ordinary cast without losing your bait) into the stained waters of my little pond.

The fascination of the pond lay in its opaqueness. I could see its surface, but what lay underneath, where the fish lived, was a mystery. Had I been able to put a boat on the pond (it was considered too dirty for swimming, and my parents made it a condition of my fishing there that I would never dive in), perhaps I could have studied its bottom, and my fascination with it would have diminished. But I never did peer down through its surface. I only experienced it from the shore, and my only connection to what lay underneath was the baited hook at the end of my line.

There wasn't a foot of shoreline where I didn't sink a forked stick into the mud and lob out my worm, and during the countless hours and days I fished there, I learned the pond's hot spots, places where the bites came more frequently, or the fish ran bigger, or the species were more interesting. I liked to try to figure out why one area produced different results from the others, and I liked trying to visualize the contours of the bottom out there, and the kinds of cover that might hold fish, and the sorts of forage that might attract them. I pictured drop-offs, holes, rock piles, weed beds. At different times of day and season, and under different weather conditions, I learned, some areas fished better than others.

So I rollcast my worm, propped my stubby South Bend rod on a forked stick sunk into the pond-side mud, stripped out an extra coil of line, and crouched there on my haunches, staring at the old yellow fly line where it entered the water, willing it to twitch to life. I did this for hours at a time, day after day, and never got tired of it.

There was nothing more thrilling than that first hesitant shudder, then the quick jerk, and then the slither of line through the guides signaling that a fish had taken my worm into its mouth. What was it? A yellow perch? A horned pout? A bluegill? A crappie? A sucker? Something more exotic, maybe, such as a largemouth bass or an eel or a carp? Or, the ultimate prize, a brook trout, a rare leftover from the year when somebody had tried stocking the place?

I'd pluck the rod from the forked stick, aim it straight down the line to give the fish a frictionless pull, gingerly finger the line, feel the life in it as it slid out over my finger and through the guides. Soon came the moment of truth when some instinct told me that the fish had my worm firmly in its mouth but had not yet swallowed it, and it was time to snug the line against the handle and lift the rod, setting the hook.

Sometimes the cheap fly rod bent acutely, but more often the lift of the rod brought a malnourished little panfish skimming to the surface.

Usually it was a thumb-sized perch or horned pout or a cracker-sized bluegill, the stunted species with which the pond was wildly overpopulated, but nothing ever disappointed me. I treasured all fish of all species and sizes. Fish were wild and mysterious and elusive. They lived where they couldn't be observed and studied, so everything I knew about them came from fishing for them and imagining their lives.

I couldn't get enough of fish. Feeling them tugging on my line, holding them in my hand, unhooking them and letting them go (I probably could have created a healthy population of panfish in my pond single-handedly if I'd killed everything I caught, but I liked knowing that lots of fish swam there; I was a confirmed catch-and-release advocate when I was in the third grade)—all of that was fun. But always the best moment was seeing that first twitch of my line that told me I had succeeded in my quest, that I had made a connection with a fish.

It's tempting to think of those countless summer hours at my muddy little pond as my apprenticeship in fly fishing, as a child's game that would evolve into something that was more important and worthwhile. Rollcasting worms into my pond did teach me how to handle a fly rod, and the feel of a fly rod loading the line became embedded in my muscle memory. After thousands of rollcasts, progressing to normal casting was a small and simple step.

It was inevitable that I'd try flies on my pond. They didn't work as well as worms, but I did catch my first dry-fly fish (a crappie about 5 inches long that sucked in a size-12 brown Bivisible) and my first gamefish on a fly (a hot-dog-sized largemouth bass that ate a Parmacheene Belle wet fly) from that pond.

But I don't think of those summers as a mere apprenticeship, as a preparation for something more exalted and valid. Lobbing worms into that muddy little pond over the hill was important for its own sake. Those were the innocent days in this boy's youth when my world was just a few surface acres big and everything important happened under the surface where it could not be seen, but could be fully and vividly imagined.

It took me all of those summers—thousands of hours, I'm sure—to learn as much about water and fish and fly casting as Lefty Kreh could probably teach me in a single afternoon. But I learned it all by myself, by trying and erring repeatedly, and so it felt—it still feels—hard-earned and important. Most fly fishermen that I know began fly fishing with, well, with flies, and with fancy equipment, and with helpful—and often insistent—instruction. Their loss, if you ask me.

My dad encouraged me to go over the hill to my muddy little pond with my can of worms and my beat-up South Bend stick, and he didn't try to teach me or caution me, and even at the time I knew enough to appreciate his hands-off philosophy.

It's been a long time since I crouched beside a pond with my fly rod propped on a forked stick. I've learned that there are many ways to be thrilled by fish, and many species of fish to thrill me. I've tried most of them, and I like them all.

It's easy in this fly-fishing passion to get caught up in complications and technicalities and fine distinctions, and why not? Fly fishing is endlessly fascinating because you can always get better at it. Nobody, not Lefty Kreh or Lee Wulff or Al McClane, has ever entirely mastered the combinations of knowledge and skill and intuition and luck that are required to do it perfectly.

But even at its simplest, fly fishing—all fishing—appeals to something inborn in all of us. I've never met a kid who didn't just naturally like fishing, and who didn't intuitively understand the straightforward physics of casting a line with a fly rod.

I was lucky to have a fly-fishing father who opened up my fishing world. He let me trek over the hill to my pond without giving me instruction or advice, but as I got older he took me to lakes and ponds and rivers and streams all over New England, too, and he showed me many different ways to entice many different species of fish to attach themselves to the end of my line.

It's been a lifelong, ever-expanding journey, with many big fish, far away waters, and dramatic moments . . . and yet I don't think any of those moments or places or fish has thrilled me more than seeing the twitch of my fly line where it entered the muddy waters of my backyard pond, picking up the rod, watching the line slither through the guides, setting the hook at just the right moment, and stripping in a thumb-sized yellow perch.

The essays here were all published, in some form, in my back-page column "Reading the Currents" in *American Angler*, or in *Gray's Sporting Journal*, or in *Field & Stream*. I am indebted to the estimable editors of those publications—Phil Monahan, Jim Babb, and Slaton White—for their guidance and encouragement and tolerance over the years. I have tinkered with many of these essays in an effort to make them fit into the general tone and purpose of this book. A writer, like a fly fisherman, never stops tinkering.

The quotations that introduce the sections are chosen, in all cases, from the writings of old friends and fishing companions. I am grateful to Harold F. Blaisdell; Ed Zern; Datus Proper; Norm Zeigler; Dick Brown; and, of course, H. G. Tapply, my dad, for their companionship and for their mentoring, as well as for their wise words.

My thanks also to Jay Cassell, my editor; Nick Lyons, my guru; Tony Lyons, my publisher; and Bob White, my favorite outdoor artist, for making it happen.

Chickadee Farm
Hancock, New Hampshire
April 2009

PART I

WHERE, WHEN, WHY

When fishermen adopt the habit of studying a book between casts, fishing will have come to a pretty pass indeed. There is little danger of this eventuality, however, for no book can substitute for experience. This is a blessing, for were such a book possible, it would take much of the fun out of the game.

—Harold F. Blaisdell, *The Philosophical Fisherman*

Fishing always reaches its peak when the bugs are thickest. And bugs are thickest in places where fishing is best. . . . So whenever and wherever you enjoy good fishing you can expect to find mosquitoes, blackflies, midges, or deerflies all lusting for your life's blood.

—H. G. Tapply, *The Sportsman's Notebook*

When fishermen come home from a day's fishing empty-creeled, and you say well, where are the fish, ha ha, they say look, bub, can't you get it through your thick skull there is more to fishing than catching fish.
But when you say what, for instance, they are stumped.

—Ed Zern, *To Hell with Fishing*

7

Are We Fly Fishing Yet?

W hen I read Rich Chiappone's delightfully venomous rant in a recent issue of *American Angler* about how Alaskan guides teach their fly-fishing clients to foul-hook rainbow trout, I was reminded of the time last May when I watched a guy with a spinning outfit catch trout from my local fly-fishing-only, catch-and-release pond during a late-afternoon midge hatch.

"Pegging," the Alaskan technique, involves stringing plastic beads onto the tippet a few inches up from a bare hook, securing them in place with a toothpick, drifting them through a pod of trout, and giving a hard yank whenever a fish nudges the bead with his nose. The hook impales the trout in the chin or jaw, the client gets to play a trophy fish on his fly rod, and the guide's a hero.

It was hard to tell what made Chiappone angrier—the unsporting nature of pegging, or the fact that they called it fly fishing.

The guy with the spinning rod at my fly-fishing-only pond had waded out to his hips right next to the beach where I was preparing to launch my float tube. In this pond, which I've found to be typical of most cold-water ponds in my neck of the woods, the hatching chironomids—and the feeding trout—start coming to the surface out in the middle. The activity gradually spreads toward the shore as afternoon descends into evening. Until the very end of it, you need a canoe or a tube to get within fly-casting range of where the fish are working.

Except this fisherman with his spinning outfit didn't need any watercraft to reach the rising trout. He winged it way the hell out there, about three of my best double-hauls laid end to end. It landed with a little splash among the dimpling trout near the middle of the pond, and he didn't wait very long after each cast before he grunted and his rod bent and he cranked in another one of the fat 15- and 16-inch brook trout that our pond is famous for.

I was mainly impressed by the gall of this guy. I could understand it if he skulked through the woods and sneaked in at the far end where he could hide if somebody like me came kicking along in a float tube. But there he stood, in plain sight, blatantly and unashamedly breaking the rules.

There's not much sense in cheating if it doesn't help you win, and I had to admit, this man sure could catch trout. He handled them carefully and released them all, too.

I watched him out of one eye while I tied a pair of midge pupae to my tippet with the other, and finally I couldn't stand it any more. "Hey," I called, "you with the spinning rod. This place is fly-fishing-only, you know?"

He looked up, smiled and waved, and then came sloshing over to me. "I *am* fly fishing," he said.

He showed me his terminal rig. He'd tied a little plastic bubble to the end of his line and about 4 feet of tippet to the bubble. A pair of midge pupae—the same choice of flies I'd made—was tied to the tippet. "Flies," he said. "See?"

A quick surge of self-righteous indignation rose and fell in my chest. I was pretty sure that this man's method violated the letter of the fly-fishing-only law. But I wasn't so sure about the spirit. The only real difference between us was that he'd found a way to drop his flies near the fish while wading in the shallow water, while I needed a float tube to reach them.

"If a warden comes along," I said, "he'll take your license."

"You think your way is more sporting than mine?" he said.

I shrugged. "I don't know."

Up until a few years ago, hundreds of fun-seekers flocked to the banks of the Salmon River in New York every fall to "lift" Chinook salmon as they staged near the estuary preparatory to their spawning run up from Lake Ontario. Lifting involved heaving a big, weighted treble hook into a mass of fish and alternately reeling and yanking. The big hooks snagged the giant fish somewhere on their anatomy, and they were then unceremoniously cranked in and heaved up on the bank.

The back-trollers and spin casters and fly fishermen who used more sporting tactics fought lifting for years before they finally got it outlawed.

When I fished the Salmon River with local salmon and steelhead guru Fran Verdoliva, we used 11-foot "noodle" rods, level 2-weight fly lines, 12-foot-long 4-pound test leaders, foam strike indicators, short droppers holding six or eight fat split-shots, and pink egg imitations made from synthetic yarn. Casting involved dangling the weighted leader and a few feet of line off the end of your rod tip behind you and heaving it like you'd throw an apple on a stick. The split shots, not the weight of the line itself, gave the cast its distance. We employed this technique—effectively—in the fly-fishing-only stretch of the Salmon River, and it never occurred to us, even as we cussed the downstream lifters for preventing hundreds of salmon from swimming up to where we might catch them, to doubt that what we did qualified as both fly fishing and ethical sport.

A few years ago a bunch of fly-fishing writers and I had to postpone an excursion to Vermont's Lake Champlain where we'd planned to cast Mickey Finn bucktails to spawning northern pike along the shoreline. We were advised, for safety's sake, to wait until after May 25 when the two-month firearms fish-hunting season ended. It was, and still is, a grand—and legal—tradition among Vermonters to climb a bankside tree or stand in the bow of a boat armed with a .30/06 rifle or a 12-gauge shotgun loaded with deer slugs and shoot cruising pike.

I've yet to meet an angler who doesn't condemn the practice of shooting fish. The shooters, however, claim that the impact of a bullet or slug on the water usually just stuns the fish, which quickly recover and swim away. Shoot-and-release, you might call it.

A Belize guide once told me that a client of his, an angler famous for his articles in fly-fishing magazines about catching permit on deerhair crab imitations, soaked his flies in the juice of crushed crabs.

I once watched a guy in the special-regulations section of the Farmington River catch trout after trout by high-sticking nymphs, I assumed, through the currents with a sweet little bamboo fly rod. It turned out he was using live mealworms impaled on a size-18 dry-fly hook.

I'm wondering where fly fishing stops and some other, lesser form of fishing begins.

Our fly-fishing ethics were codified a century ago by Frederic Halford, who condemned the wet fly, and especially the nymph. In the name of pure sport, he decreed, anglers should target only specific trout that they'd located surface-feeding on mayfly duns. The fly should float, the cast should be upstream, and the angler should be standing on the bank, not in the water.

Then along came G. E. M. Skues defending the morality of fishing with nymphs, and fly-fishing purity went all to hell in a fuzzy confusion of ends-justify-the-means relativism and hair-splitting definitions. Now we use "flies" that imitate insects other than mayflies (caddis flies, stone flies, damselflies) and fish foods other than insects (minnows, salmon eggs, crayfish, leeches). We even use "flies" that don't imitate anything at all, but are intended to exploit the fish's predatory instincts. We use flies constructed from plastics and metals and paint and epoxy. We use bobbers and sinking lines and weighted leaders . . . and still we call it fly fishing.

Fly fishing is perceived by many non-anglers as the most "sporting" method both because (they think) casting a fly is difficult to master and because it's an inefficient way to catch fish. Although neither of these reasons is valid (anybody can learn to cast, and in many situations fly fishing is the most efficient way of all to catch fish), we anglers tend to promote the illusion. It makes us feel superior and gives us good leverage for criticizing Alaskan peggers, Salmon River lifters, and Lake Champlain pike shooters—and while we're at it, all the folks who sling plastic worms and crankbaits, troll flatfish lures on wire lines, and suspend nightcrawlers under bobbers.

My father once wrote, "A man can be a fish hog with a fly rod as easily as he can with a cane pole. Easier perhaps." A man with a fly rod can also be an insufferable, self-righteous, judgmental snob. We can argue whether drifting a pink Glo-Bug and an ounce of weight under a chartreuse foam strike indicator—or casting a pair of size-22 midge pupae with a spinning rod, for that matter—qualifies as fly fishing. It's a harmless—and fruitless—debate that hinges on fine, arbitrary points of definition. Halford's concept of fly fishing remains as valid as any other.

Definitions of "sporting" are equally elusive. The Greek poet Bion wrote, "Though boys throw stones at frogs in sport, the frogs do not die in sport, but in earnest." We fly fishers need to be careful about throwing our stones at other people's ideas of a good time. Personally, I'm not much interested in lifting king salmon or pegging rainbow trout, but I confess that hunting northern pike with a deer rifle sounds kind of fun.

Opening Day 1938

The other day I was unpacking a carton of old books that my father left behind, and I paused at a nice Derrydale edition of *A Tomato Can Chronicle* by Edmund Ware Smith. I remembered how much I'd liked Smith's fishing stories. The One-Eyed Poacher was my favorite fictional character when I was a kid.

When I began thumbing through the book, I found a yellowed newspaper clipping jammed between the pages. I unfolded it. It was dated April 16, 1938.

The article was titled, "Lines Cast by 20,000 Bay State Anglers: Open Season for Trout and Salmon Begins with Limit Bags for Many Fishermen." Under the title was a faded photo. It showed three beefy men in coats and ties looking at a fourth, thinner, much younger man. The young man was holding up a dead fish that looked a bit longer than 20 inches.

I had to read the caption to identify the men: "Presenting first salmon caught to Gov. Hurley. Left to right – Edward Place, Bradbury

F. Cushing, Gov. Hurley, and Horace G. Tapley [sic], who caught the fish." My father was a very young man in 1938.

I skimmed down through the article to this paragraph: "Gov. Charles F. Hurley is not a fisherman, but he dined on a Chinook from Lake Walden at noon today in the Statler. The Chinook, one of those raised, reared, bred, and weaned at the Sandwich hatchery and dumped into Lake Walden three years ago, weighed 3½ pounds and succumbed to the streamer cast by Horace G. Tapley, magazine editor and fishing enthusiast, who with Oliver H. P. Rodman, another angler of editorial persuasions, selected Walden for the first day . . . Tapley went out in a boat on Walden about 6 a.m. and got the salmon on a light 3½-ounce rod about 8."

I had to smile. Dad used to say that he could've been elected president of the United States and still nobody would ever spell his name right. The only place his name was consistently spelled correctly was in the fishing magazines he himself edited.

I tried to imagine my old man as a young bachelor actually presenting a salmon he'd caught to the governor, and then clipping this story from a newspaper, trimming it with scissors, folding it carefully, and tucking it into a book for unborn me to find seventy years later. The father I knew mistrusted politicians (especially Democrats), shunned public ceremonies, returned all of his fish, and did not save his clippings.

But I did remember how keyed-up he would get for Opening Day of the trout season.

Fifteen or so years after my father gave his salmon to the governor, I had begun lying awake all Friday night before the third Saturday in April. He was still rising before the sun on Opening Day to drive to Walden and troll streamers with Ollie Rodman.

All the rest of the season, Dad took me fishing with him, but not on Opening Day. "Sorry, son," he'd say, "but Ollie and I always open the season together at Walden." It's an important ritual, he'd explain, a rite of passage, the true beginning of the new year, a ceremonial occasion that a man shouldn't even think of altering.

Then he'd narrow his eyes at me and say, "I hope you understand," and his tone made it clear that if I didn't understand, it was tough.

But I did understand, and I didn't mind. By the time I was eleven or twelve, in fact, I'd established my own Opening Day rituals. I dug my coffee can of worms on Friday afternoon after school and set it on the back porch along with my old bamboo fly rod and a rain jacket and my fishing vest. In the vest pockets were my envelope of hooks, my packet of split shot, my spool of leader, my folding fish-gutting, stick-cutting knife, a Hershey's bar, and a few packs of matches. In my bedroom I laid out my boots and long johns, my dungarees and wool shirt and knit sweater.

I didn't bother setting my alarm. I knew I wouldn't sleep, and anyway, Dad would bang on my door when he got up, which was around 4 AM I'd dress quickly and stumble downstairs to the kitchen, where my mother, who always seemed amused by Opening Day, would be frying bacon, and Duke, our setter, would be clacking his toenails on the linoleum floor and wondering if he had the seasons mixed up. Pretty soon Ollie would tap on the back door and then come barging in with his jokes about the weather and his predictions that he'd outfish my father.

I drank my first cup of coffee one Opening Day morning. My father told me to take it black, like a man, and I surprised him by liking it that way. Sipping a cup of pre-dawn coffee in the kitchen with the men was, I understood, part of the Opening Day ritual and an important rite of passage for me. Within a few years I'd learn that a steaming mug of black coffee before sunrise was equally integral to the rituals of duck hunting and ice fishing.

After the men took off for Walden in Ollie's wagon, my mother would drop me off at White Pond, which was just a few miles from Walden and Number Two on Thoreau's list of favorites, although the

Concord hermit wouldn't have enjoyed either pond very much on the first day of the trout season. The shorelines of both ponds were lined with fishermen, and boats of all descriptions milled around on the water.

Opening Day was a big deal back in those days. It warranted a full page of text and photos in the Boston newspapers, and people who never fished again for the rest of the year rose at dawn on that day, including politicians looking for publicity, if not for trout. On April 16, 1938, according to my father's clipping, "Ex-Gov Curley [James Michael Curley, the notorious Boston political boss], Mrs. Curley, young Francis, and Mrs. Curley's sons, George and Richard, were among the early disciples of Isaak Walton to go after the landlocked salmon and trout in Jamaica Pond. Four hours of fishing were not entirely productive for the Mayoral candidate . . ." A (staged) photo shows Curley in the bow of a boat holding a fly rod with a small, dead-looking trout (caught, one assumes, by somebody else) dangling from the end of his line. He's wearing a white dress shirt and a fedora.

I don't know how the newspaper writer fixed the number of 1938 Opening Day anglers at twenty thousand. Maybe he went to a pond such as White, counted the cars in the lot and lining both sides of the street, multiplied by two, and came up with, say, four hundred (the number he gave for Walden), and then multiplied that by the number of ponds and rivers that had been stocked. Based on my own Opening Days in the 1950s, twenty thousand was a conservative estimate.

The trick was to get there early and literally stake out a promising swath of shoreline, which I did by cutting three forked sticks and jamming them into the mud at the water's edge 5 or 6 feet apart. This marked my 10 or 12 feet of territory and gave me three spots to fish from.

My method was simple and deadly. I impaled a worm once, through the middle, on a size-8 wet-fly hook and rollcast it as far as I could (not very far) into the water. Then I set my rod in one of my forked sticks, stripped a few loops of line onto the ground, and waited, and when it began to twitch and slither out through the guides, I'd pick up the rod, count to five, and set the hook.

The best Opening Days were cloudy, misty, windless, and warm. On such days I sometimes limited out in an hour. On days of high-pressure, cold, sharp winds, and cloudless skies, it often took me till mid-afternoon to catch my limit.

I almost always brought home a limit of hatchery-raised trout, which was more than I could say for my father, a few miles away trolling streamers at Walden for the potpourri of exotic species the state stocked there in those days, including Chinook, coho and landlocked salmon, and lake trout.

Dad always seemed to get a kick out of being outfished by me. One Opening Day night I overheard him on the telephone with one of his famous fishing friends saying, "The little son-of-a-gun got his limit again, and Ollie and I trolled all day without a hit," and you couldn't miss the pride in his voice.

Somewhere along the way, the Powers That Be decreed that there would no longer be a closed season for trout in Massachusetts, and that, of course, meant the end of Opening Day, the best holiday of my childhood—and of my father's lifelong childhood—and one less photo op for the politicians.

My only regret is that Opening Day was discontinued before my own kids could celebrate it.

Just an Average Day

Last July, for reasons that don't make much sense now that I reflect on them, I stayed home while Andy and Elliot went to Paradise Valley in Montana for our—*their*, this time—annual five-day spring-creek trout-bombing mission.

After they got back home, we met for drinks so they could stick splinters under my fingernails with their stories about what I'd missed.

"Oh, it was the usual," said Andy with a shrug. "What you'd expect."

"About average," said Elliot. "You know." He grinned. "Typically awesome."

"PMDs came off every morning around eleven?" I said.

They both nodded.

"Bank sippers in the afternoon, and then the sulfurs started popping toward dark, huh?"

"Just like you remember it," said Andy.

19

"They were hard to catch," I said, "but not impossible, right? I mean, it was all about skill, not luck. Long fine tippets, careful drag-free drifts, a little experimenting to find the right fly . . .'"

"Yep," said Andy. "You had to do it all right. If you did, they'd eat. If you didn't, they'd give you the fin."

"Fish mostly thirteen or fourteen to—what, about sixteen inches? A few a little bigger than that?"

"I busted one off in the weeds, had to've been nineteen or twenty," said Elliot.

"Right," I said. "Usually one of us hooks a big one. We hardly ever land it, though. So how was the weather?"

Andy shrugged. "Typical. Bright sunny skies, temperatures in the nineties, but dry, you know, so it didn't feel hot."

"At least one afternoon thunderstorm," I said. "Double rainbow over the snow-capped Absarokas in that amazing late light. You scrambled for your cameras, but the pictures never do justice to it."

They both smiled and nodded.

"So did you try any new restaurants?"

"Nothing wrong with the old ones," said Elliot. "Inch-thick rib-eyes so big you can't find your plate, those great local microbrews."

"I remember," I said. "So you guys are saying this trip was pretty much like all our other trips. Great fishing, great weather, great food."

Andy nodded. "Just your average Montana spring-creek angling experience."

"See?" said Elliot. "You didn't miss a thing."

It's statistically predictable that most of our fishing days would fall into some kind of "average" range. We find the water level and temperature and clarity about average for that time of year. We catch an average number of fish, encounter an average number of fish that we can't catch, experience average weather, identify the expected aquatic insects hatching in about average numbers, share the water with an average number of other anglers, spot an average number of minks and herons and deer.

Unless you fish only a few times a year, pretty soon the specific memories of any particular typical day on the water begin to blur and mingle with all the other more-or-less average days until you're left with a fuzzy kind of happy feeling about fishing in general. The accumulation of all those average days defines our generalized ideas of the pleasures of fishing.

It's the aberrant, non-average times that provide us with our most vivid, specific memories, whether it's catching the biggest, or the most trout of our life, getting skunked in a drenching rainstorm, falling out of the boat, or going head-to-antlers with a bull moose who's determined to cross the river right where we're wading.

What's "average," of course, is relative to our expectations, which we subconsciously—or maybe consciously—adjust for the water where we're fishing, the time of year, the weather forecasts, and the reports from the locals.

Average for you is different from average for me. You've got your own catalog of memories and expectations.

My friends and I travel to Montana every July because an average day on a Paradise Valley spring creek would be the best day of fishing in the history of earth on one of our New England freestoners.

Every year after I get back from Montana, you'd think I'd be sated for a while. After all, I just had five 12-hour days of intense and wonderful—spring-creek average—dry-fly fishing for large trout in the most beautiful river valley in North America. I ate rare Montana beef and sipped local beers with two of my best friends. I focused my thoughts on bugs and trout and flies and tippets, and pretty soon the worries and stresses of business and money and family and health sifted out of my mind.

You'd think I had enough fishing to last me a while.

But it doesn't work that way. Instead, I barely pull into my driveway before I feel an oddly powerful urge to wade one of my local New Hampshire freestone trout streams. Something about rediscovering my roots, maybe, or restoring my perspective. I tie on a tan Elk Hair Caddis or a size-14 Adams and I run it through the pools and riffles, and on a typical evening I'll catch four or five 10- or 11-inch brown trout and miss the quick spurting strikes of half a dozen others, and by the time I reel up and start back for my car, I'll feel that I've reestablished a more comfortable concept of "average" for myself than the bloated standards I brought home from Montana.

Several years ago I caught a 16-inch rainbow from this little New Hampshire stream. A veritable trophy, and I still remember every detail of it. Here in New England, that was hardly an average evening of small-stream fishing, although measured against the Montana spring-creek scale, that rainbow would be considered a "nice" but unremarkable—and ultimately forgettable—fish.

I know a number of enthusiastic anglers who took up fly fishing as middle-aged adults. They learned to cast by taking classes at Orvis or L. L. Bean, and their first experiences on the water came in places like the Yellowstone or the Battenkill with an experienced guide at their elbow. When they decided they were hooked, they booked trips to Alaska and New Zealand and Patagonia.

These guys don't fish streams like my unremarkable little New Hampshire freestoner. Their idea of "average" is different from mine—but anyway, as they keep telling me, they have no interest in average fishing. They seek the best. They are compelled to keep outdoing themselves—and, I suspect, each other.

If I had the time and money to travel the world questing for the best fishing it has to offer, maybe I'd look at it differently, but I do sometimes find myself feeling sorry for these guys who don't really understand what "average" means and wouldn't know how to have fun flicking an Elk Hair Caddis onto the currents of a little New Hampshire stream where a 12-incher is considered a pretty nice fish.

Of course, if you look at it another way, there's no such thing as an average day of fishing. Every hour on the water, every mayfly that hatches, every fish you raise, every mink or kingfisher you see, is—or should be—a gift that deserves to be appreciated and remembered specifically, not just as blurry parts of that fuzzy happy-fishing feeling.

If you pay attention, there's always something that makes each day on the water special, that disqualifies it from being "average."

On the other hand, some days would be better if they remained average. I'm thinking of a particular Thursday last May when Marshall Dickman and I decided to meet at the Farmington River in Connecticut. We knew the Hendricksons had come and gone and the sulfurs were yet to arrive, but the forecast was for a pleasantly warm, sunny spring day, and the river was always full of fish, and we were pretty sure we'd find some of them rising in the long pool downstream from the highway bridge. Farmington brown trout were always picky to the point of aggravating, but we guessed we'd catch a few of them. We usually did. Besides, Marshall and I would have each other's company. That was always good.

In other words, we were looking forward to an average day on a river that was no stranger to us. We knew what to expect, and that's what lured us there.

Mid-afternoon found us sitting on the bank watching the water go by and trying to decide whether we should wait out the usual four o'clock doldrums, when the trout took their siestas, and hope for an evening rise, or climb into our cars and head our separate ways home.

We decided to postpone the decision by running nymphs through the long riffle under the bridge.

So we changed over to bead heads under strike indicators, and not surprisingly, we began to pick up an occasional fish.

Not surprisingly, also, I'd worked less than half of the riffle when I busted off my whole setup on an underwater rock. So I stripped in, held the end of my leader in my mouth, tucked my rod under my arm, and went prowling through the pockets of my vest.

When I went to tie on a new length of tippet, the leader I was holding in my mouth seemed to have stuck between my teeth. I gave it a tug . . . and a hunk of bridgework popped out of my mouth, plopped into the riffle, and disappeared into the depths of the downstream pool.

What it cost me to replace that dental bridge would easily finance my decidedly above-average dream trip to New Zealand's South Island.

That afternoon of trout fishing on the Farmington with Marshall last May could never be considered average. It was the most expensive angling experience in my life.

Same Time Next Year

It was shortly after the arrival of the New Year—the snow drifts around the north side of my barn stood 8 feet deep, and the red stuff in the thermometer outside my kitchen window was barely half an inch tall—when I got an e-mail from Skip Rood. In the "subject" space he had written "Second Annual Big Lake Smallmouth Trip," and it had been copied to Art Currier. It was just what I needed.

This is what Skip wrote:

> Hey Bill and Art—Time to start thinking about our second annual excursion to the Big Lake. It's never too early to get these things etched in stone. I'm looking at sometime the first week in June, which I think we've learned is when the smallmouths should be onshore and vulnerable to a well-cast Clouser or, even better, if we're lucky, a well-burbled Tap's Deer Hair Bug. You guys check your calendars so

we can zero in on a date and also a rain date. I suggest
Tuesday of that week, with Wednesday for backup, but we
can do whatever works for you. Meanwhile, tie a bunch of
flies, oil your reels, retie your leaders. I'll be tinkering with
the motor and scraping the rust off the hull of the Old
Boat.

The previous year—our First Annual Big Lake Smallmouth
Trip, I guess we can now call it, though we didn't call it that at the
time—we'd launched Skip's ancient aluminum rowboat in the last
week of May. Too early, as it turned out. Spawning urges had not yet
impelled the smallmouth bass to move into the shallow water. Along
the drop-offs in the vodka-clear lake water, when the light was right,
we could see the big females cruising near the bottom in 10 or 12
feet of water—too deep for practical fly fishing. We figured that in a
week or so we'd find them in the shallower water along the boulder-
strewn shorelines and over the gravel bars. We nailed a few of the
smaller males who'd already ventured into spawning-bed territory.
But the fishing was way slower than we all remembered it from the
Old Days.

Actually, for me, this wouldn't be the second annual Big Lake
smallmouth adventure. More like the twentieth or twenty-fifth, except
there was a twenty-year gap in the middle.

When my parents retired over forty years ago, they chose a little house
on a hillside in central New Hampshire for its proximity to excellent
grouse and woodcock habitat, and especially for the deeded access
to a sand beach on the Big Lake, where grandkids could swim and
womenfolk could sunbathe, and the fly fishers in the family could
launch a square-ended canoe.

In those days, the Big Lake saw more fishing activity when it
was sheeted with ice than after ice-out. Villages of ice-fishing shanties

sprang up when the ice was thick enough (and sometimes before—and after—that). Snowmobiles zoomed around, liquor was drunk, and lake trout, cusk, and the occasional landlocked salmon came up through the ice.

During the part of the season reserved for sensible people—from ice-out in April until the end of September—you'd see a few anglers trolling along the drop-offs for salmon. They used fly rods in the spring and lead-core lines in the summer. The Big Lake held a healthy population of landlocked salmon. Mostly, though, the lake was a playground for water skiers and speed boaters.

Access to a convenient launch site appealed to my father because he happened to know that the Big Lake was just about the best smallmouth-bass lake in New England, and he'd fished most of them at one time or another.

Best of all, nobody fished the lake for bass. We had it all to ourselves, and we hoarded our secret.

So driving from my home in Massachusetts to my parents' house in central New Hampshire and spending the weekend that followed Memorial Day on the lake with my father in his canoe became an Annual Trip. We loaded his 17-foot Grumman with two fly rods, one box of streamers and one of deer hair poppers, and ourselves, and we putted along the Girl Scout camp shoreline. We circled the islands, Dad in the stern steering the little 2-horse Evinrude and trolling a debarbed Edson Dark Tiger bucktail, and me up front, raking the shoreline with one of his deer hair bugs.

We never counted our catch or measured or weighed the fish. But my mother, who was a big fan of fishing, from a spectator's point of view, demanded a full report, and she insisted on precise numbers. So at the end of an afternoon on the lake, Dad would say, "We've got to submit a report to your mother. What do you think?"

I'd shrug. We always caught a lot of bass. "Three dozen, maybe? Four?"

"She'll suspect we're guessing if we give her an even number," he'd say. "How's forty-three sound to you?"

"Actually, that sounds very close to the truth," I'd say. "What about size? That was a nice fish you picked up off that point."

"A four-pounder," he said. "Let's call it three pounds, fourteen ounces."

And so it went, year after year, always on that same first weekend in June, for close to twenty years. I got married and had children, and when they were old enough, they joined me and my father in the canoe. Three generations of us. The first fish each of my three kids caught was a Big Lake smallmouth bass on a Dark Tiger trolled from Grandpa's canoe.

My parents grew comfortably older in their house on the hillside, the Big Lake kept producing world-class smallmouth bass fishing, and we never saw anyone else fishing there for them. It was, for me, an Annual Trip that I could count on.

Nothing is forever, of course. There came the day when Dad and I carefully fished one of our favorite shorelines and elicited just a few half-hearted swirls. It was puzzling. We could see the saucer-shaped spawning beds. It was prime time.

When we got near the Girl Scout camp shoreline, we saw that two boats were working it. They were sleek craft, built for speed, with two men perched on stools in each of them. They were peppering the shoreline with spinning lures.

There were more bass boats circling our favorite islands and other shorelines that day. We figured that the areas where we saw no boats had already been raked with treble hooks.

This was our first encounter with a bass tournament.

We turned around, beached the canoe, and went trout fishing.

That night Dad said, "No more. I'm not competing with those guys. It was good while it lasted. It's never going to be the same." And that was the end of our Annual Big Lake Smallmouth Trip.

Almost twenty years passed before Skip talked me into giving the Big Lake another try.

If this excursion to the Big Lake with Skip and Art was to become a true Annual Trip, we'd have to zero in on a regular date for it—say, the first Tuesday in June—and mark it on our calendars, not just for the forthcoming season, but for all the seasons into the foreseeable future.

I love spontaneous excursions, those times when the air smells right and the urge to fish is irresistible no matter what other plans you might've had for the day. And one-time-only adventures—trips to far-flung, exotic destinations such as (for me) Patagonia and Alaska, Labrador and Belize—are delicious to plan beforehand and to savor for years afterward.

Annual Trips are special because, well, they are annual. They come around at the same time every year. You can count on them, anticipate them, prepare for them. Fishing the same waters at the same time each year, you collect memories and accumulate wisdom. You have an idea of what kind of weather to expect, where the fish might be found, what they might be eating. Your memories of the red-letter days spice up your expectations. In the months before the Annual Trip, you tie the flies that you've learned you'll need, and you invent some new ones based on memories and theories from previous successes and failures.

One of the great advantages of establishing Annual Trips, according to Skip, is that they preempt non-fishing spouses from questioning, "Another fishing trip?" Get the dates written down in the winter. Mention the annual event in casual conversation. Weave it into the fabric of your life, like birthdays and Mother's Day.

The second Tuesday in June, as Skip had predicted, proved to be Prime Time for Big Lake smallmouths. The fish were in the shallows, eager to slash at our streamers and deer hair poppers, and although we didn't count, if I'd had to submit an honest report to my mother,

I would've said, "The three of us caught thirty-four bass. The biggest was three pounds, one ounce."

No, it wasn't the old days. The fishing was slower, and the fish ran smaller, and we did encounter three or four bass boats. But it was an excellent day on the water with old friends.

After we hauled the Old Boat out at the launch and prepared to climb into our separate vehicles, Skip said, "Next year, same time, same place, right?"

Art nodded. "Our Third Annual Big Lake Smallmouth Trip. You bet."

"Etch it in stone," I said.

Counting Coup

The first tarpon I ever cast to inhaled my fly, and when I slammed the hook into its jaw, it launched itself into the air in one of those breathtaking tarpon leaps you see in photos and believe must have been staged. It exploded from the sea like a 5-foot missile, shaking its tail and rattling its gills. Seven times it leapt, with barely a pause between jumps. It came out of the water so close to the boat that I imagined I could read the offended dignity in its big round eye. I swear it looked straight into my soul. Since I had little—okay, none whatsoever—experience in fighting 80-pound fish on the fly rod, when my tarpon decided to put distance between us, I passively held onto my rod and let it run against the drag of the reel. When my line had disappeared into the distance along with about 50 yards of backing, I could feel the big fish slogging around shaking its head, and all I could do was hold on.

You know how this story ends. Pretty soon my big tarpon was gone. It took a long time to wind all the line and backing onto my reel.

"You got to show heem who's boss," said Pancho, our Belizean guide. "Down and dirty, mon."

Now he tells me, I thought.

"You had him on for twenty minutes," said Andy.

"That's too long, mon," said Pancho. "Big feesh wear a hole in his mouth, hook come out. Too long. Get heem in quick or he get away."

"Those leaps were awesome," Andy said. "He was so close you could've touched him with your rod tip." He laughed. "Maybe you should've. You could have counted his coup."

I got my next shot at a giant tarpon in the waters near Islamorada a few years after my ignominy in Belize. Hans Carroll and I were tarpon hunting near some mangrove islands when a fish rolled beside our boat. My fly got there first, and once again we were treated to the unforgettable tarpon air show.

This time, though, when the big fish decided to make a break for it, I remembered Pancho's words. *"Down and dirty, mon."* I angled my rod parallel to the water, put my hip into it, stopped its run, turned its head, forced it left when it wanted to go right, and pretty soon I was regaining line and the fish was flashing its silver side. It was beat.

I levered the big tarpon alongside, reached out, grabbed the leader, and tried to steer it close enough that I could bring it into the boat. That was enough to inspire one last, tired thrust of its powerful tail. The leader pulled out of my hand, and before I could get the big fish back under control, it disappeared under the boat. Then it was gone.

I slumped down on the seat. It had happened again. Bested by another tarpon.

"Around here we consider that fish caught," Hans said.

"Really?"

"Touching the leader of a hooked tarpon counts as a catch," he said. "Way to go."

"I counted the big guy's coup, huh?"

"Exactly," he said. "You showed great courage. An eagle feather for you."

"I feel much better," I said.

Strangely, I really did feel better. I had failed to bring that fish into the boat. I had no photograph of myself holding it in my arms as evidence of my triumph. But I didn't consider myself a failure, as I had when my fly worked loose from the mouth of my Belize tarpon. I had counted this fish's coup, and Hans was my witness.

The native peoples of the plains—notably the Lakota and the Sioux— believed that sneaking close enough to an enemy warrior to touch him with hand or spear or coup stick was an act of great bravery and more deserving of respect and honor than killing him. According to legend, three different braves counted General Custer's coup before he was massacred (at a battlefield not far from a river where I have counted numerous brown trout coups). To count an enemy's coup is to declare: "I could have killed you, but I chose not to." It asserts your superiority. It requires more stealth and courage and skill than shooting and killing from a distance. The Sioux rewarded a brave with an eagle feather for each coup he counted.

Some Indian tribes insisted on taking the scalps of enemy warriors as proof of their superior strength, courage, and guile, much like fishermen who kill and mount their trophies.

Counting human coup is more civilized and much less messy than killing and scalping one's enemies. We count coup on tennis courts and golf courses, at poker tables and racetracks, in corporate boardrooms and courts of law.

When I was a kid, I often fished alone, with no witnesses to my prowess. Even way back then I believed in the concept of catch and release, but sometimes the question arose: If you catch a big fish but nobody sees you do it, did you really catch it? Or, to put it another way: What good is it to catch a lunker if, when you tell about it, you don't know if anyone believes you?

My solution was to kill all of the big fish that I caught. I lugged them home to show my father, who always admired my trophies and praised my angling skill . . . and then made me clean and eat the fish whose life I'd taken. Out of respect for the fish, he said.

Killing fish to win my father's praise and to prove my worthiness always left me feeling ashamed rather than proud. Pretty soon I was able to forego the praise and the need for proof in exchange for the good feeling I got from releasing a living fish back into the water.

Animal-rights, true-believers preach (with dubious scientific evidence) that catching fish by puncturing their mouths with hooks causes them pain. Fishermen think that "playing" fish is fun, but it denigrates and humiliates the fish, say the PETA people, and reduces them from noble wild creatures to our toys.

I don't quite buy it, but I get their point. More immediately, I've become aware of the numbers of fish I see floating belly-up in my trout streams after they've been caught and released—sometimes by me. Even debarbed hooks can be hard to extricate from deep in a fish's throat without injuring it. It's best for the fish's health to land and release it quickly, before it's exhausted. But lively fish twist and wiggle in your hand or net, inviting serious injury. A fly in the gills or in parts of the tongue or mouth will cause a fish to bleed, and a bleeding fish is a dead fish.

For most of us, catch-and-release is the equivalent of counting coup. It's our way of defining our victory over the fish, and it allows us to feel triumphant without taking a life. This seems like enormous progress from less than a century ago, when creels were standard equipment and fishermen were routinely photographed standing beside a dead marlin or holding one end of a long string of 5-pound native trout.

Since I found peace with the idea that touching the leader of that big Islamorada tarpon was counting his coup, I've been wondering if there's a way to improve on catch-and-release with barbless hooks. Start with the premise that the ultimate purpose of fly fishing is to "fool" the fish into taking our fly into its mouth. The high point of dry-fly fishing happens when we see a trout rise to our floating imitation. Yes, we like to hook the fish, to fight it to submission, to bring it to our hand, to remove the fly from its mouth, to cradle it in the water while it regains its strength, and then to release it and watch it swim away. If we fail to hook the fish that takes our fly, or if it breaks off or comes unbuttoned after we hook it, we are disappointed. But really, isn't all of that anti-climactic? Shouldn't the coup be counted when the fish tries to eat the fly?

If we could be satisfied with this definition of "catching" a fish, if we could forego the mixed pleasure of fighting and handling the fish we fool, we could switch to flies without hooks. Some anglers (not me, not yet) have begun to cut the bends off their flies, and they claim to get great pleasure from fishing with them.

Many veteran anglers go after tarpon with no intention of landing a single one of them. They want only to "jump" them. They like to hunt the fish, to cast to them, to induce them to take their fly, to hook them, and to witness that awesome burst of leaping. Then they shake the tarpon off or break it loose and go looking for another one.

Chad Hanson, in the title story of his book *Swimming with Trout*, describes how, while snorkeling in a river, he discovered the sport of counting trout coup. "I inched toward the fish," Hanson writes. "I held my right hand behind me and waved it just enough to keep my body in motion. It was a painstaking process, but I kept my cool until I was within two feet of the closest fish. Then my hand darted out and I gently pinched his tail."

Hanson says he hasn't sold his fly rod, and even though it sounds like fun, I don't intend to invest in a mask and fins and a wet suit. But I do aim to keep my focus on the purpose of our sport: To "touch" a fish by persuading it to take my fly into its mouth. To do this, I need to locate the fish, to sneak into casting position without spooking it, to tie on the right fly, and to present it convincingly.

That should be enough. Shouldn't it?

The Truth About Fly Fishermen

I arrived at my local trout stream just as the sun was dropping behind the trees. A pickup truck was parked in the pulloff. I stopped behind it, got out, and went to the bridge for a look. As I'd hoped and expected, spinners were swarming over the water, and the swallows were swooping around, and tiny trout dimples were showing the whole length of the long slow downstream pool.

The two men from the pickup were standing on the bank at the head of the run puffing cigars and flipping lures with their spinning outfits.

I watched them for a few minutes, then called, "How're they biting?"

"They're not," one of them said cheerfully, "unless you mean the mosquitoes."

"Mind if I fish below you?"

"Help yourself. Plenty of water."

The other guy laughed. "No fish," he said, "but lots of water."

I went back to my car, tugged on my waders, rigged up my 4-weight, slipped on my vest, and took the path down to the stream. I had to walk right behind the two spin fisherman to get to the lower end of the pool. They turned and nodded at me as I went by.

I said, "Well, good luck," and they said, "Yeah, you too, buddy. Go get 'em."

I stepped into the pool about three long double-hauls downstream from them and did what I usually do: I stood there and looked. Pretty soon I located half a dozen rising trout within casting range, and when I bent close to the water, I saw that the surface was littered with spent rusty spinners, about size 16.

Voices are muffled in the evening mist that rises from a trout stream, so I couldn't make out the actual words the two spin fishermen were muttering to each other. But I did hear them laugh, and I was pretty sure I knew what they were saying.

"One of them damn *anglers*." Spoken as if the word *angler* were a disgusting waste product.

"Dry-fly snob. Thinks he's better'n the rest of us."

"Yeah, no kidding. I heard one of them poles he's using costs over a hundred bucks."

And so forth. I'd been hearing it all my life.

The complete litany goes something like this:

Fly fishermen in general are bad enough. Even those who fish with streamers and nymphs think they're special, the way they throw back all their fish and sermonize about clean water. But the dry-fly snob is something else. You saw that movie. Dry-fly fishing is like a religion to him, like he's got the inside track on God's design. Probably has more money than God, too, with all that pricey gear he thinks he needs. He speaks Latin fluently and spends more time studying insects and worshipping the wonderments of nature than he does actually fishing for trout.

You can't talk to a dry-fly purist. If you ask him a friendly question like, "Any luck?" he'll bore you with stories about the hoary traditions of dry-fly fishing, its ancient and honored roots in England where it all began nearly four hundred years ago, where they're called "anglers," not "fishermen," and still wear tweed jackets, school ties, and plus-fours and fish by the strict rules of the river: Upstream dry flies only, cast from the bank (no wading, old chap), and only to rising trout. Which is the *angler's* way of saying, "I'm not actually catching anything, but I'm having a wonderful time."

The dry-fly snob likes to show off his skill, the years it took him to master the delicate art of the fly rod. He loves the beauty of those graceful loops his line makes as it rolls out over the water. He'll tell you he'd rather catch nothing than demean himself by using anything but a dry fly; if he does manage to hook something, he'll make that expensive rod bend as if he's hooked a monster; and if he ends up netting it, he'll turn around and let it go. He thinks he's the Ultimate Sportsman, and he fancies himself a poet. It's all about the scent of clean air, the gurgle of rushing water, the symphony of birdsong, the fine art of casting, the craft of fly tying. He loves dry-fly fishing for its ambiance, its roots, its beauty, its difficulty.

For its purity.

He's too cultured, of course, to say it, but if the dry-fly purist were to tell you what he really thinks, he'd tell you that the rest of us, those of us who just like get out of the house, catch a few fish, and have a good time, are crude slobs.

He thinks he's special. He loves the idea of being a fly fisherman more than he loves actually fishing.

The fact is he's pretentious, effete, condescending, and smug.

That's what those people are saying about us, mostly behind our backs. Now and then, toward evening. on a misty trout stream, you can hear them laughing at you.

I like all kinds of fly fishing. Actually, I like all kinds of fishing. I'm not a dry-fly purist, but it is the kind of fishing I love the most.

I've heard the snickering and the sarcasm all my life, and I've stopped apologizing and trying to explain and defending myself. It doesn't bother me anymore. In fact, I invite it.

The truth is, we dry-fly fishermen dress and talk and behave the way we do for the benefit of people like those two spin fishermen. We flaunt our expensive gear, our poetry, our aesthetics, our snobbery. We want to promote the image, to perpetuate the myth that we have the inside track on sportsmanship and that we choose to handicap ourselves with whippy little rods, flimsy tippets, tiny flies. We spurn mechanical aids like spinning reels and rely instead on timing and coordination and years of practice to put our flies near fish.

If the people who laugh at us buy into this image, we're happy, because we've got a secret, and already there are too many people who know it. The laugh's on them.

Here's our secret: We dry-fly snobs like to catch fish at least as much as the next guy. Sportsmanship, tradition, artfulness, fancy equipment, and aesthetic values have nothing to do with it.

We happen to know that any time trout are feeding on the surface, dry-fly fishing is the easiest, the deadliest—really, the only way to catch them. We can pinpoint the exact locations of specific feeding fish by their rise forms. We don't have to guess what they're eating, because we can see the bugs on the water, and we can with confidence tie on a fly that imitates those bugs. We can watch the way our fly drifts over our target fish. If we see him eat it, we lift our rod and catch him. If we see that he doesn't eat it, we know that either the fly or the drift was wrong, and we know how to make corrections.

There is no guesswork in dry-fly fishing. When trout are rising, they give us delicious, sometimes complicated, problems to solve. When we solve them, we can take full credit. Luck has nothing to do with it.

That's why we like it.

I figured those two guys were watching me, so I did what any red-blooded dry-fly purist would do: I fumbled in my fly box and retied my tippet. I scooped up a rusty spinner, perched it on my fingertip, and whispered some Latin endearments to it. I tied on a fly, doused it with flotant, frowned at it, nipped it off, tied on another one. Made a couple of false casts. Moved upstream a few feet. Fumbled in my fly box.

I played the role.

After a few minutes, the two spin fishermen reeled in and headed back to their truck. Then I false cast once and dropped my fly over one of those dimpling trout, and as it lifted its head and sucked it in, I smiled and thought: You guys with your spinning gear who sneer at my snobbery, you're the ones handicapping yourselves, throwing spinning lures at rising trout. You're the true sportsmen. We dry-fly guys, we just down-and-dirty like to catch trout.

I admit it. I was feeling pretty smug.

I fished until it got too dark to see, by which time I'd caught seven or eight of those dimpling trout. Then I reeled up, waded out, and headed back for my car.

When I climbed the bank by the bridge, a voice in the darkness said, "That was awesome, man."

Then I saw the glowing tips of their cigars. The two spinning guys were leaning their elbows on the bridge rail.

I went over. "You've been watching me?" I said.

"The whole time," one of them said. "Wanted to see how it was done. I've always thought that fly fishing was so cool but figured it was too hard for an old dog to learn. You made it look easy."

"It is easy," I said.

"Looks like a lot of fun," he said. "I gotta learn how to do that."

"Really?" I said. "You want to be a fly fisherman?"

"Yeah. I always have."

"We're terrible snobs, you know."

They both laughed as if they didn't believe me.

PART II

COLD WATER

The special thing about trout fishing with an imitative fly is that it is the only sport that proceeds from a general theory. . . . It goes like this: trout take the angler's fly because it resembles a natural creature which they are accustomed to eating.

—Datus Proper, *What the Trout Said*

At any rate, men fish for trout for reasons which can only be defined in terms of romanticism. This being the case, it is not surprising that the methods of trout fishing incorporate both practical measures and those designed to be ritually symbolic of the proper degree of devoutness. This often tends to dismay the beginner, for as intended, it conveys the impression that trout fishing is extremely complex and difficult. Since the beginner cannot distinguish between necessity and affectation, he may be overwhelmed by their sum total.

—Harold F. Blaisdell, *The Philosophical Fisherman*

I caught my first trout at the age of six, while poaching a private mountain stream in West Virginia. It was a good five inches long, and weighed upward of an ounce. I might have caught a larger one, but the owner came by and suggested I scram. He let me keep the trout to prove my prowess to my parents, but on the way back to the hotel I lost it.

—Ed Zern, *To Hell with Fishing*

Why Trout Eat, and Why They Don't

When the Hendrickson hatch is at its peak on my New England streams, the insects blanket the water. Tens of thousands of pert little sailboats come drifting on the surface, and every trout in the pool is up and slurping. This would seem to be the classic setup for match-the-hatch dry-fly fishing, but in my experience, the angler with a precise Hendrickson imitation on the end of his tippet is doomed to frustration. Your best approach is to isolate a single riser, take a position upstream and to the side of his lie, and repeatedly drift your fly downstream to him. But even that tactic generally fails. There are just too many real bugs on the water. The odds are stacked against any fish deciding to eat your fake one.

It's interesting to pick out a single trout and watch how he behaves during a blanket hatch. He sets up in the current, and even though he doesn't need to move an inch to have a shot at a steady stream of floating duns, he marks out perhaps a 2-foot-by-2-foot square of territory, and he slides up and down and side to side in that square, picking off the occasional mayfly. He selects to eat just one out of every several dozen bugs that enter his territory.

You can't help wondering about all those natural insects that this trout rejects. What's wrong with them? What's so special about those that he does choose to eat? How can an angler hope to catch this ultra-selective trout? Does it really have anything to do with the shade of pink on the fly's abdomen, or the number of tails, or the angle of the wings? Is it all about the fish's feeding rhythm?

After you've shown this trout your entire assortment of Hendrickson dun imitations, you might decide to try something different, on the theory that no imitation can look as edible as the real thing to this fish that snubs a lot of real things. Maybe a cripple, or an emerger, or a soft hackle, or a floating nymph will appeal to the opportunist in this fish. More out of frustration than because I had a sensible plan, I've sometimes ended up fishing a beetle or an Adams or a Royal Wulff to Hendrickson hatches. I've caught the occasional trout that way, too. More than once, in fact, a trout has taken my mismatched fly on the first or second cast, and I've thought, "Aha! I have discovered the secret."

Usually the next fifty casts with the magic fly produce nothing further.

When there is no hatch, we fish with what we call "searching patterns," buggy-looking flies that resemble fish forage in general without necessarily imitating any specific food item. The Adams is a standby. So are the Elk Hair Caddis, and Pheasant Tail and Hare's Ear nymphs, and soft-hackle wet flies, and Woolly Buggers. They are generalized patterns that, when presented in a lifelike manner, look a lot like many different things that drift down trout streams. We think trout mistake them for something that's good to eat, even if they don't know exactly what it is.

Another kind of searching pattern does resemble something specific that, we believe, looks familiar to trout, and they will therefore eat it even if they are not feeding actively on that forage item.

Terrestrials, for example. Streamers that imitate sculpins or crayfish. Stone fly nymphs.

Some flies are categorized as "attractor patterns." Royal Wulffs, Trudes, Stimulators, Humpies, Chernobyl Ants, Turck's Tarantulas, not to mention purple bunny streamers, red-and-white Zonkers, and Mickey Finn bucktails—flies that aren't even intended to resemble any natural trout food.

Attractor patterns, according to the theory, "attract" trout not because they look like something familiar and edible (because they don't) but because they arouse some kind of emotion in the fish. Emotions often attributed to trout are curiosity, anger, playfulness, seductiveness, bellicosity, and territoriality. Because trout do not come equipped with hands, fingers, or fists, they use their mouths to express themselves. When they bite down on an attractor pattern, they are not eating. The emotion they're responding to, according to this theory, is something other than hunger. When you tie on an attractor, your intention is to tease, seduce, or anger a trout into taking it into its mouth.

Harold Blaisdell, in his important book, *The Philosophical Fisherman*, explains it this way: "It is my belief that, in most cases, fish strike non-imitative lures for the same reason that a frog will jump for a red rag ...They do so, not as the result of normal impulses, but because of stimuli so strange that they provoke indiscretion.

"It can be argued that it is more important to know what lures fish are likely to hit than to understand why they hit them. Certainly, it is to a fisherman's advantage to be familiar with effective lures, but I think it is of even greater importance to understand the true reason for their effectiveness.

"Fishermen who use lures with the idea of provoking and arousing fish to the point of recklessness will employ shadings and touches of manipulation different from those used by fishermen trying to imitate bait fish with the same lures. And I feel certain that fishermen in the first category will take more fish. . . .

"What I have said about spoons and wobblers I believe to be true in large part with respect to plugs, bugs, spinners, streamers and wet flies that are worked or agitated. Although the success of all these lures is quite generally attributed to their imitative qualities, this claim seems extremely farfetched. Superficial inspection and observation will reveal that they resemble nothing else under the sun in appearance, and the lifelike action that they allegedly manifest is not even an approximation of the real thing. Their success, I believe, rests in their unique ability to excite fish to a state of belligerence quite beyond the control of their normal powers of discretion."

This is what we think we know about why trout eat what they eat, and why they reject what they reject: They feed selectively, or they feed opportunistically, or they use their mouths to express their emotions. Our choice of flies and tactics is based on whether we think the fish are feeling selective or opportunistic or emotional at the moment.

The problem with this entire line of thought, of course, is that we have no idea what trout think or feel. It is the height of anthropomorphism to assume that fish experience anything remotely resembling what we humans know as anger, for example. When we use terms like "selective" or "opportunistic" or "belligerent," we're not really *explaining* the fish's behavior—we're simply *describing* the way it looks to us.

There's no good reason to assume that trout have feelings at all, never mind feelings that are similar to human emotions. It's quite likely that trout don't "think," if by that we mean that they use their brains to sort out the variables in their lives, to speculate about their futures, and to devise plans for solving their problems. Trout exhibit an array of behaviors that have evolved over eons to enable them to survive as individuals and to procreate their species. It's safe to say that these behaviors are instinctive, perhaps refined by some life-experience conditioning—but not the product of reasoning. The trout's brain does not intercede between the sudden appearance of a fisherman's shadow on the river bottom and the fish's quick dart to deep sheltered water. Nor does the trout think about what it selects to eat or to pass up. It reacts.

Thomas McGuane, in *The Longest Silence*, understands the trout's selectivity this way: "In my view, a trout that is feeding selectively is doing the following: having ascertained that many of the objects going by his view are edible, he decides which ones he can eat efficiently and which will do him the most good. Then, in the interest of energy conservation, and if the chosen food item is in sufficient quantity, the trout gradually transfers the decision-making process to something like muscle memory, to thoughtless routine. If the fly we cast fails to trigger that recognition or is not in the rhythm in which the trout is feeding, we get a no-sale."

I think McGuane is right about "muscle memory" and "thoughtless routine," but I'm pretty sure that trout "ascertain" and "decide" things differently from the way we humans do, just as they feel "anger" and "belligerence" and "fear" differently from us, if they feel those emotions at all.

Ed Zern, who for many years wrote the back-page column, "Exit Laughing," for *Field & Stream*, gets the last word on the subject of why trout eat what they eat and why they reject what they reject: "Of course, every once in a while a fly fisherman catches a trout on a trout fly, and he thinks this proves something. It doesn't. Trout eat mayflies, burnt matches, small pieces of inner tube, each other, caddis worms, Dewey buttons, crickets, lima beans, Colorado spinners, and almost anything else they can get in their fool mouths. It is probable they think the trout fly is some feathers tied to a hook. Hell, they're not blind. They just want to see how it tastes."

When Trout Get Antsy

Aquatic insects, in their many and varied species and in all the stages of their life cycles, provide food for trout and hatch-matching problems for anglers. Sometimes it's deliciously challenging. Frequently, though, it can be downright infuriating, as Elliot Schildkrout and I discovered one hot August day on a big western trout river.

The morning spinner fall had come on schedule, shortly after daybreak. But it fizzled out under a blazing Rocky Mountain sun, and by midmorning it seemed as if every trout in the river had gone back to bed. We rowed slowly downriver, scanning the water for rising fish. Finally we spotted a few noses poking through the slick currents that the river funneled against the base of a high bluff. We pulled the driftboat against the bank.

"Oh, yeah," whispered Elliot reverently. "Look at that."

Dozens of trout were sipping quietly tight against the steep bank. When we looked at the water, we saw Trico and *Baetis* duns and spinners; black, speckled, and blond caddis flies; Yellow Sally stone flies; and several species of midges drifting on the surface. It was a trout smorgasbord.

"What do you think they're eating?" I said.

"Anything," said Elliot, already climbing out of the boat. "Everything. It's a buffet. Let's get 'em."

We fished side-by-side, changed flies often, called the fish colorful names, and raised no trout, although they continued to feed off the surface—sometimes within millimeters of our imitations.

After a while I accepted defeat. I reeled in, climbed into the anchored boat, and took a sandwich and a jug of lemonade from the cooler. While I ate, I watched Elliot, more persevering than I, continue casting, changing flies, and mumbling. Bugs kept crawling on my face, and I brushed them away. One got in my mouth, and when I spit it out, I must have muttered a curse, because Elliot turned and said, "What'd you say?"

"Damn ants," I said. "They're all over the boat, in my face, on my sandwich."

"Ants, huh?"

The next thing I knew, his rod was bent and his reel was screeching. He landed the trout and a moment later had another one on. That's about when I figured it out.

Ants. They ruined my picnic, but they were the trout's banquet.

We should have known. Whether they're rising selectively to a hatch of aquatic insects or gobbling opportunistically at whatever comes their way, trout rarely refuse to eat the odd ant that drifts over them. A good trick to taking selective fish during a heavy mayfly hatch is to show them an ant imitation. Even when they're not rising at all, you can often take trout on a floating or wet ant pattern. The ant is the closest thing to an all-purpose trout fly that I know.

If you look closely, you'll see ants crawling on virtually every square foot of land in the world where trout streams flow, so it's not surprising that ants drift on every brook, spring creek, tailwater, and freestone river in North America. They continually fall or get blown onto the water. Midges, mayflies, stone flies, and caddis flies come and go. But trout see ants all season long, and they eat them constantly.

Anglers have speculated that trout find the ant's distinctive formic acid taste addictive. According to legend, Edward Hewitt, intrigued by trout's obvious fondness for ants, popped a few into his mouth and chewed them to see if he could understand their appeal. He made a face and declared that ants tasted bitter.

In fact, Hewitt's discovery happened accidentally when a couple of winged ants flew into his mouth, and he never claimed it was their taste that explained why trout were so attracted to them.

Most likely it's the ant's distinctive pinch-waisted appearance that becomes imprinted on the trout brain. Trout learn early that ants are a staple, a food source they can absolutely depend on for nourishment. The ant's shape makes it an easily recognized target on the water.

Despite their ubiquity and trout's fondness for ants, many fly fishermen seem reluctant to use ant patterns. Even the most experienced anglers of my acquaintance, who know how much trout love ants, generally tie one on only as a last resort.

It's not hard to understand. Dry-fly fishing at its best is a visual experience. We like to be able watch our fly drift toward a rising fish. We hold our breath as the distance between floating fly and rising trout narrows. The sight of a trout snout lifting out of the water to intercept a dry fly is what keeps us coming back.

A properly imitative ant pattern, on the other hand, floats low in the surface film where it offers the angler no visible silhouette. It's drab and tiny and hard to see on the water.

And fishing an ant properly seems technical and fussy. Especially in low-water mid-summer conditions when they are most effective, ants require long (12- to 15-foot) leaders and fine tippets (6X or even 7X). They must be presented with an absolutely drag-free drift, and even then, energy-conscious trout will rarely move more than a few inches from their feeding station to eat the tiny morsel. Trout seem to know that there will be plenty more ants coming their way.

When I've located a feeding trout in smooth shallow water, I compensate for the visibility problem by sneaking up behind it. I approach from directly downstream. I wear drab clothing, wade cautiously, keep a low profile, and as I approach the fish's position, I don't hesitate to kneel-walk on the streambed. If I move slowly and carefully, I can often creep to within 15 or 20 feet of my target trout. From that distance, with good polarized glasses I can usually see my leader tippet and the fish himself—and sometimes, on smooth water, even the speck of a size-20 ant. I try to make short accurate casts, and I watch how the fish reacts to my fly.

In broken water, I don't even try to follow the drift of my ant imitation. Instead, when I see a trout rise in the vicinity of where I think my fly is, I gently but firmly lift my rod, on the theory that nothing ventured is nothing gained—or, as my friend Bill Rohrbacher says, "No guts, no glory." More often than not, I come up empty, and sometimes pulling the fly and leader off the water spooks the fish. It's a reasonable risk for the reward that comes with the thrumming surge of a surprised trout at the end of my line.

The visibility problem can also be solved with a strike indicator. Cut a little piece of foam stick-on indicator (the smaller the better, since the air resistance of full-sized commercial indicators inhibits smooth accurate casting with small flies and fine tippets) and pinch it onto the tippet knot, about 3 feet from your fly. Don't watch the indicator or wait to see it twitch before you set the hook—that's usually too late. Simply use the indicator to help judge where your fly is on the water, and raise your rod whenever you see a fish rise in that area.

A standard dry fly also works well as an ant locator. Tie a size-16 or size-18 Wulff or Elk Hair Caddis to your tippet, knot 3 feet of 6X tippet to the bend or the eye of that fly, then tie an ant pattern to the end of the 6X. The odd trout that rises to the dry fly itself is a bonus.

About fourteen thousand species of ants crawl on the earth's surface. They come in a bewildering variety of colors—black and cinnamon are the most common, but I've seen dark brown, bright red, pale yellow, and even bi-colored ants floating on trout streams. They range from $\frac{1}{16}$" to more than an inch in size. As many as a dozen different species can be present on the water at any one time. So even when you've figured out that trout are eating ants, matching the "hatch" can seem impossible.

Fortunately for the fisherman, while trout often feed on ants in preference to the other insects available to them, they rarely select one specific species of ant to the exclusion of the others. Sometimes they may favor black over red, and sometimes size makes a difference. But usually I've found them opportunistic. When trout want ants—as they generally do—almost any size and color imitation will take them, provided it offers that distinctive wasp-waisted profile.

When a swarm of flying ants falls on a stream, on the other hand, trout can be as infuriatingly selective to size and color as they are to mayflies. Trout feed voraciously on flying ants. But usually the fisherman must match the hatch, or he'll catch no fish.

Luckily, flying-ant falls are predictable. They typically occur in late summer on warm, humid, windless afternoons. The well-prepared angler learns from experience what to expect and comes prepared with a selection of flying-ant patterns customized for his waters.

Both winged and wingless ants are terrestrial insects. Their appearance on the water, while common, is always accidental. They cannot swim, so they drift helplessly, borne afloat by surface tension, before they sink and drown. In riffled water, where they sink rapidly, subsurface ant imitations are especially effective. Fish them without weight just a few inches deep to imitate the real things.

Floating ant imitations can be made from a variety of materials—cork, deer hair, closed-cell foam, and dubbing, with a couple turns of clipped or bunched hackle for legs. All are effective provided they are designed to drift flush in the surface film rather on top of it. Add a pair of laid-back hackle tips and you've got a flying ant. To make sinking ants, simply form lacquered balls of tying thread for the bodies. The key to imitating ants is reproducing their large oval abdomens, narrow waists, tiny legs, and round heads.

Ants are notorious for ruining picnics. But when they're on the water, as they usually are, they provide a buffet for trout—and a trout-fishing banquet fit for an angling king.

Dam It

Until a few years ago, I'd lived my entire life in eastern—which is to say, suburban—Massachusetts. This part of the world is famous for its institutions of higher learning, its Green Monster, its high-tech industries, its liberal politics, and its intimidating traffic circles, which locals call "rotaries" and out-of-towners liken to Russian roulette in automobiles.

Conversely, virtually nothing has been written about the trout-fishing opportunities in eastern Massachusetts—not because there are well-kept secrets, but because there are no such opportunities worth mentioning. Some of the scummy streams that flow behind strip malls and through culverts support populations of stocked trout for a month or two in the spring, until the heat and drought and toxic runoff get them. Most of the ponds, regardless of water quality, are stocked, and the fishing can be quite fast in April and May if you've got a good hatchery-pellet fly and don't mind a lot of competition.

Then, at last, I moved to southwestern New Hampshire, a hilly, heavily forested and sparsely populated region that fairly bubbles with cold, clean water. Every crease in the earth flows with a river, stream, brook, or rill. Big lakes and small lakes and millponds and kettle ponds fill every depression. The first year I lived here, I was a starving man all by myself at a lavish buffet. I flitted from stream to pond to river to brook, and everywhere I fished I found trout. And best of all, maybe—I rarely saw another fisherman.

So why, in the second week of the second July of my residency in this New Hampshire trout paradise, did I buy myself a non-resident Massachusetts fishing license?

Because my New Hampshire streams had withered and shriveled in an extended June drought, as freestone streams sometimes will do. I needed cold, moving water. I needed healthy trout to cast to.

I needed a tailwater, and there were none in my part of New Hampshire.

But there were two just over the border . . . in Massachusetts.

The Swift and the Deerfield rivers in western Massachusetts were actually closer to home now than they'd been when I lived in suburban Boston, and I fished each of them several times that summer, whenever the urge to wade cold water and cast to husky, insect-eating trout got the best of me.

And each time I crossed the border, I was reminded of how dependent I'd become on dams for my trout-fishing pleasure.

In my family, the word "dam" didn't need an "N" on the end of it to be a curse. We worshipped any landscape that a river ran through. The Army Corps of Engineers, which apparently existed for the sole purpose of stopping water from running freely, was the devil's army. My father believed that the army corps built dams because the rivers were there and that's all they knew how to do. He called the corps "serial killers."

Dams on the great New England rivers that once flowed freely to the sea—the Connecticut, the Merrimack, the Penobscot, the Kennebec, and on virtually all of the lesser oceangoing rivers and streams, too—blocked the spawning runs of the Atlantic salmon and, in effect, extirpated this great gamefish.

My father believed that fish were more important than factories, and as a kid, I absorbed his religion and made it my own. As I explored my local brooks and streams, I noticed that virtually all of them had been dammed, and that mills and various other waterworks had been built at the sites. Inevitably that's where villages sprang up. In my hometown, one millpond sat on the site of a Civil War gunpowder factory and another next to an abandoned pencil factory. Many New England villages grew up around water-powered mills that ground corn and other grains or ran sawmills. Even today, you'll find very few New England towns that some river or stream doesn't run through.

Dams on bigger rivers powered turbines that supported textile and paper factories. Cities appeared here.

In all cases, free-flowing rivers and streams were halted, diverted, and manipulated for the power that the water-plus-gravity equation provided. The water that flowed over the tops of the dams into the river that resumed downstream was always the warmest and least oxygenated. The fish suffered accordingly.

Hating dams, of course, is like hating progress, or hating civilization, or hating people. It's easy and satisfying and justifiable depending on how you interpret your information. When I was a kid, I liked fish better than people. That was part of my family's religion.

A neighbor of mine here in New Hampshire, an early-retired CEO named Chuck with more money than he knows what to do with, not an angler but a nice guy nevertheless, kept inviting me to fish for the trout he'd introduced into the swimming hole he'd built for his grandchildren on his south pasture. I kept making excuses.

Catching pet trout from a swimming pool didn't interest me. But he kept mentioning it, and finally my wife suggested that I couldn't make excuses forever. I should either just say "no" or get it out of the way.

I took the easy out and showed up one afternoon with my 4-weight and a box of flies. The rectangular "pond" covered about half an acre. Chuck said it was fed by water piped up from the aquifer and stayed cold year round. He'd stocked it with one hundred Kamloops rainbows that now had grown to about 16 inches on the special fish food he gave them.

A few dragonflies flitted around the edges of the pond. I saw no bugs on the vodka-clear water, nor did I see any sign that a fish lived there. Chuck was watching me expectantly, so I tied on a small black Woolly Bugger—if anything lived in this hole in the ground, it would be leeches—and cast it halfway across the pond. Let it sink. Twitched it back. Nothing.

Chuck was frowning at me as if I were an incompetent fisherman, and after a dozen or so futile casts, he said, "Watch this." He produced a coffee can of grayish-beige pellets and cast them upon the water, which almost instantly began churning and flashing with hungry fish.

I found a size-16 Hare's Ear nymph in my box—a fair imitation of a specially formulated, multi-vitamin fish pellet—tied it on, cast it out, let it sink, saw my leader twitch, came tight, and caught a very strong Kamloops rainbow from a man-made swimming hole in southwestern New Hampshire.

Chuck was pleased that I caught a trout from his pool. I was pleased to have fulfilled that social obligation. My wife was pleased that I didn't offend Chuck or, especially, his wife.

The experience reminded me of the reasons I love fishing. It's to transcend man-made things, to encounter wild creatures on their own terms, to leave civilization and to enter, as a predator, the natural world. Catching fish assures me that I'm an effective predator, and I need that once in a while. Otherwise, it's about fishing, not catching. It's about Being There.

And yet . . .

I delude myself. I'm a hypocrite.

By actual count, nine of my personal top-fifteen favorite trout rivers are man-made. They're as synthetic as Chuck's swimming hole.

They are tailwaters, coldwater rivers that flow from the bottoms of giant dams where once warmwater rivers flowed.

Aside from a few spring creeks and a couple of freestoners, my most beloved rivers wouldn't harbor a single trout were it not for man's willingness to corrupt the natural landscape for the sake of hydropower and flood control and crop irrigation and drinking water. They are: the Bighorn (created by the Yellowtail Dam), the Green (Flaming Gorge Dam), the Missouri (Holter Dam), the Frying Pan (Ruedi Dam), the Norfork (Norfork Dam), the Farmington (Colebrook Dam), the Swift (Windsor Dam), the Deerfield (Fife Brook Dam), the White (Bull Shoals Dam), and the San Juan (Navajo Dam).

Tailwaters, by definition, are fed by the consistently cold and fertile water that is released through the dams from the bottom of the reservoirs.

These rivers are angling destinations. They hold dense populations of large trout, they produce lavish and predictable hatches of mayflies and caddis flies, and they can be fished year-round. In many cases, trout fishing has supplanted power generation as the most lucrative product of the dam. Whole towns spring up around these rivers, with fly shops and boat rentals and outfitters, not to mention hotels and restaurants and gift shops, whose income depends on visiting anglers.

In spite of their artificial origins, tailwaters are infinitely interesting. No two pose the same challenges. Each has its own unique combination of water temperature, oxygenation, and fertility, each riverbed had its own characteristics, and each dam releases and holds back water according to its own—generally unpredictable—schedule. Insect populations vary. The sizes and densities of the resident trout differ in each tailwater, too.

Once I learned to turn my back on the dams, those towering engineering monstrosities that give tailwaters life, I experienced some of my most memorable days of trout fishing—and catching—on these man-made rivers.

Sometimes I feel like a traitor to my father's damn-the-dams religion. But Dad never fished any of the great tailwaters. If he had, I like to think that he was enough of a Yankee pragmatist to join me in my comfortable hypocrisy.

Out of Season

When I was growing up in Massachusetts, the trout season opened on the third Saturday in April and closed on the last day of September. As much as school vacations, Christmas, and my birthday, the annual opening and closing of the trout season shaped the rhythm of my year. I celebrated Opening Day, fished hard and often all summer, and counted down those dwindling September weeks to the Last Day. Fishing was a warm-weather activity. Venturing to a river or pond in the fall or winter would've felt unnatural even if it had been legal.

Many years after I'd internalized these annual cycles so that they had become my own biorhythms, Massachusetts eliminated the closed season on trout. Suddenly you could cast for trout anytime.

Not me. The law had nothing to do with it. I had no desire to go fishing between the last day of September and the middle of April.

When that changed—as, of course, it inevitably did—and the idea of fishing in the fall or winter no longer felt criminal to me, I traveled to warm places like Florida and New Mexico, Argentina, and Belize.

Fishing in the northeast out of season, as I still thought of it, held no appeal for me. New England weather in those months ranged from mildly unpleasant to downright miserable. Besides, any trout that had managed to survive through the summer spent the cold seasons resting their bellies on the bottom like waterlogged driftwood waiting for warming water to inspire them to eat. You could always go fishing; catching was another story.

So when Phil Monahan called me in the third week of October and asked if I wanted to go trout fishing, my, "Yes, of course. I always want to go fishing," sounded feeble and unconvincing to my ears.

Phil apparently didn't hear me the same way. "Excellent," he said. "This'll be fun."

"Where?" I said. "What've you got in mind?"

"A float trip," he said. "On the Deerfield River in western Mass. It's like floating the Madison or the Yellowstone. These brothers, Tom and Dan Harrison—Harrison Anglers, they call themselves—they earned their chops guiding in Montana and Chile. They've been floating the Deerfield for several years now. They think it's as good as anyplace they've been."

"The Deerfield, huh?" This interested me. I'd fished the Deerfield River dozens of times over the years. It was a big brawling tailwater, with a healthy and self-sustaining population of browns and rainbows. The Deerfield was a big-fish river, and when I'd managed to hit it on low or falling water, I usually had good dry-fly fishing.

But I'd only seen the Deerfield by wading the few accessible areas that I could find. Much of the upper several miles flowed through deep gorges and thick forests far from any road. The chance to experience the river from the inside out, so to speak, and to fish water that wading anglers such as I couldn't reach, was enormously appealing.

We agreed to meet at the Charlemont Inn, on the banks of the Deerfield, at 9 AM two days before Halloween.

"Bring your six-weight," said Phil. "We'll be throwing Glo-Bugs and split shot, and maybe streamers. Don't forget to wear layers. You never know about the weather this time of year."

Prophetic words. When I left my house in southwestern New Hampshire the morning of our Deerfield float, the woods and fields lay white under the first snow of the season. Roiling gray clouds hung low in the sky. The temperature, according to my car thermometer, was 34 degrees.

I'd dressed in layers, and I brought my 5-mil neoprene duck-hunting waders, and woolen gloves, and a knit hat, and two pairs of socks. I figured I'd end up chilled to the bone anyway.

Tom and Dan skidded their rafts down a steep slope not far down from the river's beginning at the Fife Brook Dam. Dan rigged me up with a pair of Glo-Bugs, several split shots, and a big strike indicator. The reservoir was full and the river was running high. "High water pushes the fish up against the banks," he told me as we eased into the flow. "Fishing from rafts, we love high water."

Dan rowed hard to keep us in position against the persistent, chill wind that was blowing directly downstream. Pretty soon it began to snow, and the wind grew teeth.

From my front seat in Dan's raft I lobbed my indicator-Glo-Bug-split-shot setup along the current seams and mended it through the slots and steered it against the brushy banks. Now and then my indicator would dart down, and I'd lift my rod and come up tight for a second. "Gimme a look at your fly," Dan would say, and sure enough, we'd discover that I'd left tippet and split shots and Glo-Bug on an underwater rock or sweeper, and patient Dan, whose fingers were no doubt as numb and chilled as mine, would rig me up again.

This, of course, was why they'd made autumn trout fishing illegal when I was growing up: Because otherwise anglers might actually go fishing, and they needed to be protected from their own dumb enthusiasm.

After an hour, our only excitement was seeing the indicator twitch and dip. I busted off the whole rig several times.

I was chilled, yes, and the trout weren't cooperating. But I was hardly miserable. Experiencing the Deerfield this way, drifting between the steep timbered slopes of the gorge and through the rocky rapids and down the side channels, with no sign of human life except our two rafts, but many signs of wildlife, I was transported back to other big wild rivers I'd floated—sections of the Yellowstone and the Missouri in Montana, the Box Canyon of the Henry's Fork, the Green River in Utah and the Bow in Calgary, the Class-4 rapids of the Rangitaiki on New Zealand's North Island, and, especially, the Middle Fork of the Salmon River in Idaho where it cuts through the Frank Church River of No Return Wilderness.

You don't need to be holding a fly rod to be utterly captivated by a wild river.

After a while Dan dropped his anchor. He pointed. "There. That current seam."

On my third or fourth drift through the slot, my indicator dipped. By now I was a little gun shy. I hated the idea of busting off yet again. But when I lifted my rod, this time I felt the throb of a fish, and a moment later Dan netted a pretty rainbow of maybe 13 inches. "There are bigger ones down there," he said. "The browns are starting to spawn, and the 'bows hold below them, sucking up their eggs."

The next time my indicator disappeared, I came up hard on something big and strong. "Good fish," I grunted.

A minute later Dan laughed, and then I saw what he saw. I had another average-sized rainbow, but I'd hooked this one in the tail. Tail-hooked trout pull hard.

A couple of drifts after that, when my indicator twitched, I felt power at the other end of my line, and when the fish rolled, Dan said, "Oh, yeah."

It was a fat, yellow-bellied brown with spots that looked like drops of fresh-spilled blood. Dan measured it against his net. "Seventeen inches," he said. "A worthy trout anywhere."

Dan told me that his and Tom's clients had caught trout up to 24 inches long from the Deerfield. "We don't guarantee you'll catch a two-footer," he said. "But they're here. In the summer when the high water pushes the fish against the banks, we drift dry flies along the bushes, and the biggest fish in the river are there, waiting to eat. When conditions are right, we have some really big days on this river. As good as any fishing in the Rocky Mountain West."

We stopped for lunch on the sheltered side of an island. Phil and Tom joined us. We ate thick ham and turkey sandwiches, and compared notes. Both boats had taken several fish. We all agreed that the Deerfield, with snow spitting from dark skies, felt wild and starkly beautiful.

After lunch I resumed drifting my Glo-Bug rig along the current seams near the banks. When I predictably broke off on an underwater log, I asked Dan to tie on a streamer for me. I couldn't bear asking the man to keep rerigging the complicated Glo-Bug setup anymore.

Dan shrugged. Reading his body language, I guessed he didn't have a lot of faith in streamers today. But I was quite sure he was sick of tying knots with numb fingers. He selected a white Matuka. It looked good in the water.

Throwing streamers, double-hauling, stripping, lifting and casting again got my body moving. The blood began to recirculate through my extremities. It felt good.

Then my fly stopped, and when I strip-struck, I felt a heavy weight.

"Hey!" said Dan.

It was a hefty 17-inch brown, a twin of my earlier fish.

Then I had another hard hit, and then another, and during the hour or so that we floated after lunch, I must have had ten solid hits and several swirls. I hooked a few, landed two, and when Dan nosed the raft onto the bank at the takeout and I stepped out, the wind was driving the snow horizontally down the river.

But I felt almost warm, and I realized that I had a new attitude about out-of-season trout fishing in New England.

Tuna Fish Sandwiches and Other Inert Materials

High noon on the Bighorn. The August sun was blazing down from a cloudless Montana sky. The morning Pale Morning Dun hatch had petered out, so Andy and I pulled our driftboat against a high bank and tossed the anchor up into the grass. I sat in the stern seat, catching some shade from an overhanging cottonwood and eating a tuna fish sandwich. Andy, who considers eating a waste of precious fishing time, climbed out and began stalking a pod of sipping trout upstream from where I sat. I was admiring his stealth when a soft slurping noise made me turn to look behind me.

A good-sized rainbow trout had moved into the eddy created by the anchored driftboat, about 20 feet downstream from where I sat in the stern. As I watched, his head twisted to the side and his mouth winked white. A minute or so later he did it again.

Idly I broke off a bit of tuna from my sandwich and dropped it into the water.

The trout moved into its path and sucked it in.

I fed that trout several bites of my sandwich. Each time he ate, he finned a couple of strokes upstream, moving closer to the source of this tasty new nourishment, until he hovered almost in the shadow of the boat.

Why not? I thought.

Moving very slowly lest I spook him, I picked up my rod, unhooked the #18 PMD dry fly from the keeper ring, and impaled a piece of tuna on the hook. I dropped it over the side. As it drifted toward the trout, a little surge of current caught the leader and jerked it sideways, and he turned away to let it pass. I stripped some line off my reel, shook some extra slack out through the guides, and tried again. The trout ignored it as it passed over his head.

So I dropped my tuna-PMD a bit farther upstream and guided it so that it drifted directly to the trout's nose. This time he opened his mouth and ate it.

I remained sitting in the stern as I played, netted, unhooked, and released him.

"Nice one," yelled Andy, who had turned to watch. "What'd he take?"

"Nothing you've got in your fly box."

I was, I admit, a bit embarrassed. Catching trout on bait—even something as exotic as a chunk of white albacore lightly dressed with mayonnaise, salt and pepper, and ginger hackle, and impaled on a size-18 dry-fly hook tied to a 14-foot leader tapered to 6X—is generally thought to require luck and patience, not skill and knowledge. Most of us would rather be considered skillful than lucky. Bait-fishing is for barefoot boys with cane poles and worms and more time than skill—which, presumably, is why grown-ups give up dunking bait in favor of casting flies.

And yet . . . to catch that big rainbow, I had to locate him, avoid spooking him, and present my bait so it would drift to him in a perfectly natural manner—all of which required the same skills that fly fishermen value.

"Okay," I said to Andy. "It was a short cast but a tricky presentation. He took a tuna fish sandwich. And I'm proud of it. You got a problem with that?"

"Nope. I think it's kinda cool." He grinned. "You know, even with your expensive graphite fly rod and your fancy neoprene waders, you're still a barefoot boy at heart."

Back when I *was* a barefoot boy, the only fishing outfit I owned was a hand-me-down 8-foot South Bend fly rod, a Pfleuger Medalist reel, and a kinky HDH floating line. I could cast, if that's the word for it, anything with that rig—bass bugs, streamers, dry flies, spinners, miniature Jitterbugs. Mostly, though, I fished with worms. Trial and error taught me how to rollcast so that the worm would not come unhooked, and how to lob a bobber or split shot a considerable distance.

When I fished for trout in our lazy local brooks and streams, an unweighted worm on a fly rod usually did the job. I figured out how to flip the worm up into the head of a pool and steer it through the fish-holding lies. I intuitively understood the importance of keeping my line off the water so that the worm would tumble along with the currents. I had never heard the word "drag," but I could have explained it to you. I watched the place where my leader entered the water, and the slightest hesitation or twitch triggered my hook-setting reflex. Sometimes it meant I'd hung up on a rock or sunken log. More often, it was a trout.

In heavy currents, it made sense to clamp a split shot or two onto my leader to get it down to where I figured the fish were lurking. I wanted to feel the lead bounce and tick off the bottom. The fish I caught that way told me when I was doing it right.

Back when I was a barefoot worm fisherman, I kept most of the trout that I caught. When I cleaned them, I liked to poke through the gunk in their digestive systems. Most of it was unidentifiable, but I always found bugs in their various stages of metamorphosis—nymphs, pupae, larvae, and adults. The scientific studies I've read confirm my personal, non-scientific conclusions. Aquatic insects make up about 95 percent of most trouts' diets. The remaining 5 percent is comprised of small fish, crustaceans, and what the scientists call "other inert materials," stuff like pebbles and twigs and cigarette butts.

I don't recall ever finding an earthworm in the belly of a trout I caught on a worm, nor do the scientists report that earthworms are a significant part of trout menus.

And yet the history of fishing proves that trout eat worms whenever they come tumbling along—not to mention San Juan Worms (which theoretically imitate aquatic worms), Glo-Bugs (which anglers like to believe "imitate" salmon eggs, but which I've found effective in waters where no salmon live, and in mid-summer, when no fish of any description are spawning), and inert materials such as feathers and fur arranged on fish hooks to resemble—at least to the angler's eye—mayfly or stone fly nymphs.

Why do trout eat earthworms—and twigs and pebbles and Glo-Bugs and tuna fish sandwiches? Why, for that matter, do they eat our clever imitations of subsurface aquatic insects? In the case of worms and tuna, perhaps it's because they smell edible—although in neither case can the odor be familiar to the fish.

Glo-Bugs, San Juan Worms, and nymphs, we like to believe, look like actual trout food. When we catch trout on these lures, we congratulate ourselves on successfully "fooling" them by imitating what they like to eat.

When trout are feeding selectively, as they sometimes do (though probably less often than we think), it may help to imitate what they're eating. Most of the time, though, I believe any barefoot boy who can drift a worm—or even some inert material such as a Glo-Bug or San Juan Worm—onto a trout's nose without drag, will catch it. Trout use their mouths the way we use our hands—to feel and test and explore their world. They are always hungry and always curious, and they'll bite down on anything that looks remotely edible.

I'm pretty sure that Bighorn rainbow had never eaten canned albacore tuna before I shared my sandwich with him. But he was curious, and it probably smelled good. So he tried it, and he liked it, and he looked for more. Still, when I impaled a piece of tuna on a hook, he refused to eat it until I managed a perfectly drag-free drift.

I suspect I could have caught him on a nymph or Glo-Bug or San Juan Worm or some other inert material, too. But I'm rather pleased that I persuaded him to eat a piece of my sandwich. It reminds me that I haven't forgotten what I learned as a barefoot boy.

Fear of Midges

Back when we were just starting out as trout fishermen and couldn't get enough of it, Art Currier and I would pick the first likely weekend in late March or early April to break our winter famine. We'd lash my canoe onto the roof of Art's station wagon and head for Cape Cod, where the ice melted off the ponds several weeks earlier than on our local waters. We'd paddle around the shoreline of Scargo or Flax or Peters, trolling Mickey Finn and Dark Tiger bucktails, and we generally caught enough trout to make us happy.

If we had one of those particularly delicious, gray, misty days—a "soft" day, we called it—the wind would lie down entirely and the pond's surface would go as flat as a black mirror. Then, almost always, the trout would start rising. Hundreds of trout. Thousands, maybe. Every fish in the pond, it seemed. It looked like hailstones were falling all over the surface. These were not the splashy, energetic rise forms we were accustomed to seeing on our New England freestone streams. They were dainty sips, trout just kissing the surface, mere pockmarks on the flat water, and the first time we saw them, we assumed they were made by chubs.

We took this phenomenon as certain evidence that our pond was full of hungry fish, and the fact that we seemed to catch way fewer of them when they were rising like this than when they weren't didn't discourage us. Once in a while one of them would latch onto a bucktail, but typically we had our worst luck when the fish were most actively and visibly feeding.

When the breeze kicked up again, our luck usually improved, so that was our strategy: Wait for some wind.

In those days, Art and I were both just starting at the bottom of our fly-fishing learning curves. We figured a pondful of feeding trout should hit any fly they saw, and when they didn't, we shrugged, called it bad luck, and kept on trolling.

We had no first-hand experience with selectivity. It made no sense that hatchery-reared, pellet-fed brook trout would discriminate among all the edible stuff they might find in a pond. All we knew was that they ate trolled bucktails almost anytime, just like the stocked fish in our streams seemed happy to gobble any bushy dry fly that drifted over them.

Looking back, it seems stupid that we didn't purse our lips, exchange meaningful glances, mutter "midges," add 2 feet of 7X tippet to our leaders, and tie on some fly the size of a comma. We'd read about midges, and we knew that they were ubiquitous on our New England trout waters. If those writers were to be believed, midges were important trout food.

So why, when the pond went flat and the trout began rising, didn't we try to figure out what they were eating? Why didn't we lean over the gunwales of my canoe and study the water? Surely we would have seen that its surface was scummy with buggy specks, and if we'd only picked one up on a fingertip and studied it, we'd have seen that it had a simple black body and a pair of laid-back transparent wings, and we'd have concluded that *this* must be what all those trout had come to the top to eat, and, based on our poor success in catching them, that they had targeted midges to the exclusion of everything else, including trolled Mickey Finn bucktails.

I suppose we were arrogant in our ignorance. Maybe we were just incurious. We were certainly inexperienced, and we were suspicious of all the highfalutin theories we read in books and magazines. We scorned those writers who spouted Latin and verbally dissected insects and debated arcane details of fly color and design. We thought they gave the trout way too much credit. They seemed to want to make it all more serious and complicated than we knew it really was. Trout fishing was straightforward and simple.

We didn't believe in midges.

So we just kept trolling.

Art and I learned from our fathers, whose own fly-fishing learning curves spanned the 1930s and '40s, when the tiny insects that we now know trout thrive on were neither understood nor appreciated. Vincent C. Marinaro (one of those fishing writers that Art and I, regrettably, sneered at), in his important 1950 book, *A Modern Dry Fly Code*, wrote: "In those early days [before World War II] I could not take advantage of the marvelous small-fly fishing that prevailed on the limestone waters, simply because I did not have the tools for the job. I was frequently galled to the core when I found good trout feeding incessantly on minuscule insects for hours on end and I could not make a fair try for them because I did not have flies small enough or gut fine enough to handle them properly. The very small hooks in sizes 22, 24, and 28 and very fine gut in 6X, 7X, and 8X were not available."

Marinaro was way more observant and persistent than most anglers, and he lived on a lush limestone meadow stream (the Letort in central Pennsylvania) that gave him an ideal trout laboratory. He virtually discovered minuscule trout food (he misspelled it "minutae")—midges, jassids, ants, beetles, and *Baetis* and Trico mayflies.

Most fishermen—I include my father and most others of his generation—didn't even notice these nearly microscopic insects, and they would have rejected their importance if they had, simply because without fine tippets and tiny hooks, the information had no utility. It was, in that respect, arcane and worthless.

Most anglers—including, belatedly, me—discovered the importance of minutiae only after we had the tools to imitate it.

My laboratory was the Swift River, a tailwater that empties the Quabbin Reservoir in central Massachusetts. The waters of the Swift run frigid year round, and its bottom is mostly sand and silt and mud, making it inhospitable to mayflies. But when I started fishing there, I was entranced by the fact that I always found large rainbows feeding off the surface. Those fish had no interest whatsoever in my usual assortment of dry flies. I just couldn't catch them, and I was forced to look closer—closer than I'd ever bothered to look before.

I saw drifting on the Swift what Vince Marinaro saw on his Letort: ants, small beetles, and especially midges. What else, thought I, could those trout be eating?

It fascinated and obsessed me, these big fish eating such tiny bugs, and I haunted the Swift. For the first year or so I refused to give in to them entirely. The idea of using a floating fly that I couldn't see offended me, and I doubted that it would work. So I compromised, fishing with beetles and ants in sizes-16 and -18 on 5X tippets, smaller and finer than I liked to go, and I began to catch some trout.

I was converted entirely one soft March afternoon when I found every fish in the Y Pool sipping off the surface, and I couldn't interest a single one of them. I bent close to the water and saw midges. Really tiny black midges, barely half as long as one of my size-18 ant imitations.

On the way home I stopped at a shop and bought packets of size-24 dry-fly hooks, and that night I squinted through the magnifier on my vise and fabricated my own version of those Swift River midges:

four or five fibers of black deer hair lashed down at the back, folded forward, and tied off behind the hook, with the tips cut to length and flared like legs. It was a simple—simplistic, really—fly, more suggestive than imitative. But the size and the color were about right, and to my eye it more or less resembled what I'd seen on the water. The next day, when I went back, the trout agreed. I caught half a dozen of those hefty 16- to 18-inch rainbows on flies that were utterly invisible to me.

What I'd always loved about dry-fly fishing was the visual: watching a high-floating fly drift down to where I'd seen the swirl of a rising fish, anticipating the intersection of fly and trout, then seeing the fish poke up its nose, open its mouth, and suck in the fly.

This midge business was different, and in its way, even more thrilling. Marinaro said it best: "To see a trout rising to something invisible, to fasten a diminutive No. 22 dry fly to the gossamer point and cast that fly to the trout, judging the accuracy of the cast by following the line, to see the gentle swell of the rise again when the obscure No. 22 should have floated over the desired spot, then to tighten and discover the connection with a lunging trout is the most exotic experience that can befall a fly fisherman. Let it happen a thousand times or ten thousand times, the novelty of the event never palls, never loses that quality of breathless expectancy."

My Love Affair
with Spring Creeks

I fell instantly, passionately, and irrevocably in love on the sun-drenched summer morning more than twenty years ago when I saw my first Montana spring creek up close.

It emptied into the Yellowstone River just south of Livingston. The jagged Absaroka Mountains, still snow-capped in August, filled the sky. Warblers and finches flitted in the willows and cottonwoods that lined the banks, and swallows and waxwings swooped low over the water. Whitetail deer tiptoed down to the banks to drink. Paradise Valley, they called the area. And no wonder.

I stood knee-deep in the chilly water. It flowed slow and slick, braiding and eddying subtly around patches of green water weeds. Flotillas of Pale Morning Duns were drifting all around me. Within easy casting range, a dozen large trout snouts were lifting rhythmically to suck them in . . . and I couldn't persuade a single one of them to eat my fly.

A lifetime of casting to naive hatchery trout on eastern freestone streams had not prepared me for this. This spring-creek fishing, I thought, was the Real Thing. I found it utterly addictive.

I've returned to Montana every summer since that day twenty-odd years ago, and I've always scheduled a day or two on one of the three legendary Paradise Valley spring creeks—Armstrong, DePuy, or Nelson. On a few heady occasions I've accepted invitations to try lightly fished creeks that flow through private ranch land.

Healthy spring creeks provide ideal trout habitat. Their consistent year-round temperatures encourage trout to feed and grow large through all four seasons. They are fertile, fostering lavish weed growth and heavy populations of aquatic insects and other trout forage. Spring-creek trout eat insects their whole lives. You can catch truly monster spring-creek trout on tiny dry flies.

I've learned that every spring creek has its own style and personality. They are big and small, wide and narrow, shallow and deep, swift and slow, straight and twisting. In some creeks, the trout are sparse and small and skittish; others harbor dense populations of snooty big ones. Each creek presents its own challenge.

I love them all.

Spring creeks and the savvy wild trout that thrive in them always test my skills. They continue to make me a better angler.

Montana trout guide Bob Bergquist estimates that about nine hundred spring creeks flow through his state. Virtually every river valley is laced with them. Montana river valleys make prime farm and ranch land. Spring creeks feed the cattle and irrigate the crops and infuse the major river systems with cold, clear water. They range in size from trickles to full-sized streams. Most of them harbor some trout.

But left to their own devices—and to the uses of ranchers and farmers—few spring creeks are worth fishing. Because they generally rise in land with little gradient, their nature is to flow straight, flat, slow, and shallow. Their bottoms become silty and produce few aquatic insects. They offer meager cover or spawning habitat for trout.

Various state and federal conservation agencies provide landowners with consultation and incentives for improving spring creeks. Bergquist estimates that about one hundred Montana creeks have been, or are in the process of being, "improved." They are dredged to remove silt and create trout-holding holes. They are narrowed and bent and twisted to create gravelly riffles and quick-moving runs. Rocks and logs add eddies and pools. The banks are fenced and planted with willows to protect them from cattle.

Most improved creeks are privately owned. Some can be fished if you know the landowner. Such a creek flows through the property of the late Datus Proper in Belgrade. Datus labored for years with heavy equipment to make it a lovely, productive—and challenging—trout stream. It has an official name, but Datus called it "Humility Creek." I can vouch for the fact that he named it aptly.

Recognizing the value of good trout water with restricted access, some ranchers lease the fishing rights to their creeks to outfitters. Lately, Montana entrepreneurs have begun building housing developments around spring creeks, much like Florida communities are laid out around golf courses. A stretch of Baker Creek in Bozeman, for example, has been improved under the supervision of the legendary Montana angler and outfitter Bud Lilly. Buy a house lot in the development and you can fish this pretty little creek whenever you want.

There are just a few fishable public spring creeks in Montana. Two of the best ones—Poindexter Slough in Dillon and Big Spring Creek in Lewiston—hold decent populations of trout and feature good mayfly hatches. But overfishing and overcrowding are significant negatives on all public trout waters, and especially on intimate spring creeks.

For decades, the Nelson, O'Hair, and DePuy ranching families in Paradise Valley have offered anglers first-come-first-serve, restricted-access, year-round, pay-to-fish angling on their marvelous creeks. For about a hundred bucks per rod, you are guaranteed an uncrowded day of high-quality angling for large, challenging trout amid glorious surroundings. I have always considered it a bargain.

In recent years, two other Montana ranch families have improved their creeks and adopted similar formulas. A few summers ago, Bob Bergquist introduced me to the creeks on the McCoy ranch in Dillon and the Milesnick ranch in Belgrade. They were lovable.

In the early 1980s when Poncho and Bev McCoy began ranching cattle on their two thousand acres in the Beaverhead Valley near Dillon, the two spring creeks that meandered through their property had been neglected and degraded by years of use and abuse. They were shallow and silty and barren of cover, and few trout lived in them. So Poncho, a former Olympic skier and an enthusiastic fly fisherman, went to work. He dug ponds, he dredged holes, he narrowed channels, he added boulders, he cut what he calls "squiggles" into the creek beds, and he converted rather sterile water into prime trout habitat.

In 1996 the McCoys opened one of their creeks and several ponds to public fee fishing. They opened the other creek to anglers in 2001. Today, their 3 miles of spring creeks and their ten small ponds are full of large, healthy, insect-eating, self-sustaining brown, rainbow, and brook trout.

I explored the McCoy creeks with Bergquist and a few friends for several days toward the end of June a few years ago. We rented the comfortable guesthouse right there on the ranch and fished ten or twelve hours a day.

Except for one blustery morning when I threw Woolly Buggers into a pond (and nailed several big rainbows), I had no reason to cast anything but dry flies. Sharing a one-and-a-half-mile beat of delicious spring creek with just one or two other anglers, I was able to find and stalk rising fish all day long.

Midges hatched in the mornings and evenings, and Pale Morning Duns came off sporadically in the daylight hours. These relatively lightly fished trout were not overly selective. If I covered them with a drag-free drift and a reasonable imitation, they usually ate. Black foam beetles worked all day long. On the ponds, the fish crashed adult damselfly imitations.

Trout that live in shallow water flowing through open flatland survive by remaining alert for predators, including two-legged ones waving sticks. Careless wading and sloppy casting spooked them every time. I wore drab clothing and spent a lot of time on my hands and knees.

The trout, predominantly rainbows, averaged around 16 inches. We caught many in the 18- to 19-inch range.

Truly monstrous brown trout inhabit the McCoy creeks. I spent the better part of one afternoon stalking what appeared to be a large fish that I'd spotted cruising a flat and sipping an occasional insect from the surface. He finally opened his mouth and sucked in the Comparadun that I'd cast 12 feet ahead of his anticipated path. He had a snout like a northern pike and measured 25 inches.

That fish was no fluke. The chances of catching a giant trout on a small fly at McCoy's are legitimate. The week after I left, Bergquist told me one of his clients took a 27-incher on a beetle from the same flat where I caught my big one. An album in the guesthouse holds dozens of photos of anglers grinning behind the 30-inchers they're holding up for the camera.

Poncho and Bev McCoy are committed to maintaining the quality of their fishery. They divide the creeks and ponds into two "beats" and restrict each beat to two or three anglers. Fishermen are urged to use barbless hooks, land fish quickly, handle them gently, and return them unharmed to the water. The McCoys close their ranch to fishing from October 1 to March 31 to protect spawning trout. During these months, Poncho continues to dredge, narrow, and add boulders and squiggles to his creeks. It can only get better.

A similar success story has played out in Belgrade, just a ten-minute drive from the Bozeman airport. There, on 1,400 acres of prime Gallatin Valley ranch land, the Milesnick family has been raising cattle since the 1930s. Two lovely spring creeks—Benhart and Thompson—meander through the property for 3 miles before they empty into the East Gallatin River. Over the years, savvy local anglers caught an occasional big fish from the creeks, but decades of overgrazing had left them mostly silty, wide, and shallow, and trout populations were sparse.

In the mid 1990s, Tom Milesnick, recognizing the fish-holding potential of his creeks, set about to restore them. He dug pools, narrowed channels, created riffles, points, cutbanks and bends, planted willows . . . and the trout moved in. Simultaneously, the Milesnicks developed an innovative grazing system that restricted and controlled their cattle's access to the water and kept the creek banks stable and streamside vegetation lush.

A few years ago, both to limit the fishing pressure and to finance their restoration work, the Milesnicks opened their waters to the general public on a fee-paying basis. "Challenging" was the word I kept hearing.

A few summers ago I accepted the Milesnick challenge.

The Milesnick creeks, I soon learned, aren't for everybody. In these intimate, smooth-flowing waters, the fish are as wild and spooky as any I've ever cast to. They demand long, fine tippets, drag-free drifts, careful casting, patience and stealth—and a good sense of humor. If you don't think of it as "challenging," "frustrating" might be your word of choice.

One afternoon when I was taking a break in the fishermen's shelter, Tom Milesnick stopped by. He asked how I was doing. I told him that his fish were giving me a good education.

A smile spread across his leathery face. "Couple fellas who came this morning just drove away," he said. "They were pretty mad at my trout."

Besides the two spring creeks, the Milesnick spread offers 5 miles of private access to the freestone East Gallatin River, where challenged or frustrated anglers can rebuild their egos with more cooperative trout.

I swear that in two days on the Milesnick spring creeks I became a better trout fisherman. I learned to go slower, look harder, creep more quietly, and strategize my approach to every fish. The mostly 16- to 17-inch rainbows—plus one memorable 20-inch brown—told me I'd done everything right when they lifted their heads and confidently sucked in my fly. Every hooked fish felt like a triumph.

The way I look at it, that is the ultimate in trout fishing.

PART III

WARM WATER

For the life of me, I cannot give bass their due and equate them with trout. I come closer to full appreciation whenever I can take bass on a fly rod, and I think there is good reason to prefer fly fishing for bass above all other methods. Explosive surface strikes add greatly to the thrills, and bass hooked on bugs or flies can give much better accounts of themselves than those punished and encumbered by the multiple hooks of plugs and spoon.

—Harold F. Blaisdell, *The Philosophical Fisherman*

I really think that the largest bass will come to the largest bugs, especially at dusk, at night, and particularly before there's any light on the water in the very early morning.

—Nick Lyons, "The Bass Fly Revolution," *Field & Stream*

Large-mouth bass hang around stumps and lily pads, passing the time of day. Small-mouth bass prefer rocky ledges. Ask them why and they hem and haw. Paradoxically, small-mouth bass fishermen tell bigger lies than large-mouth bass fishermen.
Incidentally, the flavor of a large-mouth bass is vastly improved by popping it into the garbage can and going out for dinner.

—Ed Zern, *To Hell with Fishing*

Bass-Bug Humbug

"It is with some degree of trepidation that I approach the subject of artificial flies [for bass]," wrote James A. Henshall in his *Book of the Black Bass*, "for I am afraid that I hold some very heretical notions on the subject. But of one fact I am positively convinced, and that is, that there is a good deal of humbug on this matter."

Henshall published his classic book in 1881, and the humbug has been proliferating ever since—especially about fishing for bass on the surface with the fly rod.

Thumb through a fly-fishing catalog or wander the aisles in your local fly shop and you'll be astounded by the number and variety of bass bugs. There are poppers, chuggers, sliders, and divers made from deer hair, balsa, cork, and foam in myriad sizes, shapes, colors, and designs. Many are impressively lifelike representations of actual bass prey (fish, amphibians, reptiles, insects, mammals, worms, and even baby birds), and they come with imitative appendages such as wings, legs, arms, tails, gills, fins, antennae, whiskers, and eyes. Many offer additional options such as propellers, rattlers, lips, and weed guards.

These bugs are designed to catch fishermen, not bass.

The unwary bass bugger might feel compelled to buy several of everything in a full range of sizes and colors on the theory that you never know what the bass might want, and you better be prepared to imitate it. Many books and countless magazine articles have been written about the challenge of fooling selective bass and the importance of tying on the "right" bug.

Humbug.

The truth is, both largemouths and smallmouths will come to the surface to eat any old bass bug just about anytime, anywhere. If they don't, it means they're either not there or they're in no mood to eat, and you might as well go home.

Trout, as we know, can be infuriatingly selective (although I have caught a lot of big ones on bass bugs that looked like nothing in nature).

Bass are full-time predators. They're opportunists. All they want is something—anything—that looks alive and easy to capture and nourishing, and that's the only thing a bass bug needs to resemble.

To be sure, some bugs are decidedly better than others. But what they imitate is the least of it. Tie on whatever you want, cast it to the right places, and rest assured, if there are hungry bass nearby, they'll eat it.

If you want to buy or make a good bass bug, don't fret about what it looks like. There are more important considerations, such as:

☐ **Aerodynamics.** Besides catching bass, the great fun of bass-bug fishing is identifying and casting to all those delicious targets that line a bassy shoreline—the pockets among beds of lily pads, the half-submerged trees, the dark holes under overhanging bushes, the shadows alongside boulders and docks. A badly designed bug (air-resistant wings and tails and other appendages, general bulkiness) quickly makes your casting arm ache and sucks all the fun out of it. Choose a light, streamlined bug that you can cast comfortably with a medium-weight (5- to 7-weight) rod. If you can't find such a bug, you can improve the aerodynamics of a bulky bug with scissors.

☐ **The burble.** The sound of prey moving on the water's surface, more than its shape or color, is what convinces bass to strike. You should be able to impart a variety of lifelike noises to a bug. Give it a sharp tug to make it go *ploop.* A twitch makes it burble, and with an erratic retrieve it chugs, glugs, and gurgles. You can create the widest variety of seductive noises with deer hair bugs.

☐ **The flutter.** Effective bass bugs are never entirely motionless. Even at rest they shiver, shudder, quiver, and flutter. A sparse, hairy tail and a few rubber legs improve any design.

☐ **The plop.** Actual bass prey fall upon the water with a muffled *splat* or *plop.* If your bug lands soundlessly, nearby bass won't hear it. If it crashes to the surface, they'll flee. Closed-cell foam and deer hair bugs make the best plop.

☐ **Floatability.** Like typical bass prey, good bugs float in, not on, the surface. But they should float all day. It's hard to impart lifelike motion and noise to a bug that rides too high on the water, and it's frustrating to have to change bugs because the one you've tied on has started to sink. Poorly designed hard-bodied bugs (cork and balsa) float too high. Loosely packed or insufficient deer hair soon becomes waterlogged and sinks.

☐ **Hookability.** The gape of the hook should be wide relative to the size of the bug or else you'll miss a lot of strikes. Keep your hook points needle sharp. Mash down the barbs.

☐ **Size.** Under normal conditions, the size of the bug is not crucial. I've caught 5-pounders on bugs meant for bluegills, and 12-inchers on bugs the size of sparrows. Something on a size-2 hook for largemouths and a little smaller (size 1, say) for smallmouths is about right. Nick Lyons writes evocatively about the way big bulky bugs attract big bulky bass at twilight, and they surely do, although Art Scheck argues that those same bass would probably gobble panfish bugs that you can cast comfortably on a 4-weight trout rod. I think they're both right and take the middle ground. On flat, shallow water, oversized bugs might scare bass. On choppy water, though, the commotion of a big bug helps to attract them.

☐ **Shape.** Bass guru Will Ryan chooses stubby bugs for shoreline fishing and sleek, tapered bugs for offshore reefs and shoals. He theorizes that bass expect to find wounded and disoriented baitfish offshore and terrestrial creatures near the banks, so he picks bugs whose shape suggests, but needn't imitate, the predominant bass prey. This is a good theory, and it works for Will if for no other reason than it gives him confidence in whatever bug he ties on. When it comes to shape, though, the important criterion is still how well the bug casts.

☐ **Appendages.** Keep them sparse and soft for good castability and quivery motion on the water. Most commercial bugs are severely over-dressed. Eyes and ears serve no function except to attract fishermen, since bass can't see the top of a bug from beneath it.

☐ **Color.** Frogs are green, baitfish are silvery, moths are white, mice are gray. All of these colors make good bass bugs. So do purple and chartreuse and pink and blue. From a bass's viewpoint— looking up at the belly of a floating bug—it's just a blurry silhouette. A spot of red on the bug's "throat" might suggest flared gills and trigger a bass's predatory impulse, and a pale belly resembles the undersides of most bass prey. Otherwise, because it doesn't matter to the fish, the best bass-bug color is whatever you can see best on the water. I like yellow and white.

☐ **Durability.** Bass are toothless creatures. A good bug should survive the chomps of a dozen or more fish. The material it's made from is less important than how well it's made. The cork, foam, or balsa bodies of poorly made bugs can come loose and slide up and down the hook shank or even break off. Badly spun deer hair bodies will fray, twist, become waterlogged, and fall out. If you make your bugs yourself, you can attend to the details that make the difference. If you buy them, you can't be sure.

☐ **Weedlessness.** Bass, especially largemouths, lurk in and among lily pads, reeds, and other aquatic vegetation. A bug that slithers around, through, and over weeds and half-submerged tree branches and snags allows you to cast to the places where the big ones live. Weed guards are generally made from monofilament or wire. Bugs tied on keel hooks theoretically ride with the hook bend up. I've never owned a completely weed-proof bass bug. The annoying rule of thumb seems to be: The better they prevent snagging weeds, the worse they hook bass. I usually avoid weed guards entirely and take my chances unless casting among dense weeds is my only choice. Then I use bugs with monofilament loops tied along the bend of the hook and just behind the eye. This design is somewhat weedless and hooks bass pretty well. It's the best compromise I've found so far.

☐ **Materials.** Spun deer hair, closed-cell foam, or hard (cork, balsa, plastic)—each has its advantages. I prefer deer hair. It makes delicious *plops*, *ploops*, and *burbles*. I imagine it feels like something alive in the mouth of a bass, it floats low in the water, and, when well made, it endures a day's worth of chewing and chomping. I happen to enjoy spinning and trimming deer hair, which is not an inconsiderable factor. Closed-cell foam is hands-down the easiest material to work with. I can make half a dozen functional foam bass bugs in the time it takes me to make one good deer hair bug. If you like cabinet making—carving, sanding, gluing, and painting—rather than fly tying, by all means make your bugs from cork or balsa.

Each material has its small advantages and disadvantages, but all are minor compared to what the angler does with his bug— casting it close to shadowy shoreline targets on a soft summer's evening, imparting enticing sounds and movements to it, and strip-striking hard when the water implodes and a big bass sucks it in.

Mr. Bass

Twenty years ago I got a phone call from a stranger that transformed my life.

"My name is Andy Gill," he said, "and I want to take you fishing."

At that time I had a nine-to-five job and a wife and three little kids at home. I fished when I could, which was nowhere near as often as I liked, mostly with my dad, and never farther away than I could get to and back home from in a day.

Andy mentioned a mutual friend—a guy named George—and then I remembered George mentioning Andy to me. Andy, George had said, was some kind of hotshot bass fisherman. He belonged to a club, owned a fancy boat, competed in tournaments. In fact, Andy was the reigning club champion, which had earned him the title Mr. Bass.

"You're Mr. Bass, right?" I said to Andy.

"Oh, jeez," he said. "That's embarrassing. So how's a week from Thursday work for you?"

A week from Thursday was the Fourth of July. My family was expected at a neighborhood cookout that afternoon. "I'd have to be home by noon," I said.

"That's okay. We should be on the water no later than five. We'll have a super morning, I guarantee. I got a great place in mind. Secret spot. Big bass. Meet me here at my house at four." He gave me directions. He lived on the other side of town. "See you then, right?"

His enthusiasm steamrollered me. "Okay," I said. "Sure."

Mr. Bass was sitting on his front steps sipping coffee when my headlights shone on him at four o'clock Thursday morning. A pair of aluminum crutches lay on the ground beside him, and his right leg from toes to knee was encased in a white cast.

I got out of my car, went up to him, shook his hand, and said, "What happened?"

"Ruptured my Achilles tendon. Driveway basketball game. Happened about an hour after we talked the other day."

"You still want to go fishing?" I said.

He rolled his eyes. "You kidding? I always want to go fishing. You gotta drive, is all. Throw your gear in the truck and let's get going."

I had brought my usual bass-fishing outfit—a medium-action 8-weight fly rod, a reel loaded with a floating forward-taper line, a spool of 2X tippet, a tube of flotant, and a box of deer hair bugs.

A sleek bass boat was trailered behind Andy's truck. It had two swivel seats and a live-well. A 50-horse Honda outboard hung off the transom. A little electric motor and an electronic fish-finder lay on the floorboards.

I'd never ridden in a real bass boat.

When I stowed my stuff in the back of Andy's truck, I saw three tackle boxes the size of suitcases and at least a dozen rods of various lengths and designs.

Andy hobbled over and hoisted himself and his crutches into the truck. I slid behind the wheel. "I never drove a trailer before," I said.

"Nothing to it," he said. "Let's go. Fishing's best before the sun hits the water. Step on it."

I drove through the darkness and Andy gave directions, and twenty minutes later he said, "Right up there's the ramp. You gotta back down."

I'd watched fishermen back trailered boats down a ramp to the water plenty of times. It looked easy.

But it wasn't.

Finally, Andy got out, leaned on his crutches, and shouted and waved directions at me. By the time I managed to steer the trailer into the water, unhook the boat, get my fly-fishing stuff plus all of his rods and tackle boxes transferred, and park the truck, the sky was beginning to brighten in the east and Andy was stumping around on his crutches muttering, "Let's *go*, let's *go*, let's *go*."

I stood there looking at the water. I'd been so intent on following Andy's instructions as I drove his truck through the night that I hadn't paid much attention to where we were going. "Wait a minute," I said. "This is the Charles River, right?"

"Yep."

"The Waltham Watch Factory is right over there." I pointed into the darkness. "My grandfather worked there during the Depression."

He nodded. "Urban angling."

"It used to be great for largemouths," I said. "But last time I fished here it stank so bad I couldn't stand it. Dead water. No fish."

"When was that?"

"Close to twenty years ago, I guess."

"They cleaned it up," he said. "You'll see." He cocked an eye at the sky. "Let's go fishing, okay?"

I smiled. "Okay."

"You know how to run an electric motor?"

I shook my head. "I've never been in a bass boat before."

"I'll do it, then. You've driven outboards, I hope."

"Sure."

I helped Andy and his crutches onto the pedestal seat up front. Then I shoved us off, took the stern seat, and ran the outboard.

I steered us up the broad, barely moving river for a couple of miles, following Andy's signals, and killed the motor at a bassy-looking cove when he pointed and held up his hand.

He turned on his electric motor and selected a baitcasting rod from his arsenal.

I grabbed my fly rod, tied on a deer hair bug, and fingered some Gink into it.

"Bass bug, huh?" said Andy. "Good bait."

"Easy decision," I said. "It's the only, um, bait I ever use for bass. What're you using?"

"Jig-n-pig," he said. "I got a hundred options."

Andy, up front in the bow seat, raked all the likely spots in the cove with his jig-n-pig bait before I had a chance to burble my deer hair bait over them, but the first fish of the morning sucked in my bug.

"Hey," said Andy. "Okay."

I lip-landed the fat 2-pounder, backed the barbless hook from the corner of its mouth, and slipped it into the water.

A few minutes later I caught another bass about the same size.

Andy muttered, "Humph," then stowed his jig-n-pig outfit and selected another rod.

"Now what're you using?" I said.

"Stickbait."

His stickbait was a surface lure. Pretty soon a bass hit it. It came unbuttoned on a jump. It looked like a big one.

"Nice fish," I said.

Andy grunted and resumed casting. Grimly, I thought.

We had no more action there, so he directed us to another cove.

This one was rimmed with overhanging bushes and littered with blowdown and patches of lily pads.

"Wow," I said. "Classic."

"My secret spot," he said. "I anchored my boat and won a tournament right here a few weeks ago."

A 3-pounder ate my second cast, and a few minutes later I caught one that Andy estimated at close to 5 pounds. He had one half-hearted swirl at his stickbait before he switched again.

"What's that bait?" I said.

"Spinnerbait. If this doesn't work . . ."

A few casts later I caught another 3-pounder on my now-bedraggled deer hair bug.

When I released it, Andy put down his rod. "You realize," he said, "that you've caught five nice bass and I haven't caught any?"

I shrugged. "I wasn't counting." I cocked my head at him. "I wasn't competing, either."

"You didn't change baits once," he went on as if I hadn't spoken. "You just kept throwing that bug close to the structure and made it go *ploop* and *burble*. You'd have won most tournaments with those five fish."

"Structure," I said. "Bait. Vocabulary words."

"Meanwhile," he went on, "I'm changing baits, changing rods, changing tactics, applying all my hard-earned tournament-tested skill and wisdom, and I hook one measly fish. And he throws the damn bait."

"Largemouths are simple fish," I said. "They'll eat anything. It's all just luck."

"If it was all luck," he said, "would I be Mr. Bass?" He turned on his swivel seat and grinned at me, letting me know that he didn't take any of that stuff all that seriously. "You got another one of those deer hair baits?"

"It's a bug," I said, "not a bait. You got a fly rod?"

"I've got three fly rods here in the boat," he said, "and about two dozen more at home. I've got three pairs of waders and a hundred boxes of trout flies and salmon flies and steelhead flies and saltwater flies, too. You think this is the only fishing I like?"

I shrugged. "I didn't know. You are Mr. Bass."

He rolled his eyes. "I don't think I'm gonna live that down. Listen, seriously. You been to Montana?"

I shook my head.

"Alaska? Labrador? Patagonia? Belize?"

"No," I said. "I dream about those places."

"Want to?"

"What? Go?"

He nodded. "Next summer. A week in Montana. You owe it to yourself. I'm not taking no for an answer, okay? The Bighorn. The Yellowstone. The Madison. The spring creeks. You with me?"

I gazed up at the sky for a moment. Was I with him? It seemed like an important question.

I looked at Mr. Bass and nodded. "Yes, sir, I am. I'm with you."

The next summer Andy and I went trout fishing in Montana, and we've been doing it ever since. Belize, Labrador, Alaska, Patagonia, too, and many, many fishy places in between.

As I said, that phone call twenty years ago transformed my life.

Somewhere along the way, Mr. Bass let his club membership lapse, sold his bass boat, and crammed his baits and tackle boxes and spinning and baitcasting rods into a closet, where they've been gathering dust ever since.

The Perfect Fish

The little pond covered no more than ten surface acres. Its wooded banks sloped sharply and were overhung with thick brush. Lily pads grew in the shady coves. Here and there, an old oak tree lay half-submerged in the water. Frogs grumped and burped from the shore, and neon dragonflies and damselflies darted around, and . . . well, it looked as good as the rumor that had lured us there.

The rumor: Big largemouths that had never seen a bass boat. Access limited to a long winding path through the woods. Strictly carry-in.

Doc and I had toted in his little 13-foot aluminum canoe.

Doc won the toss and elected to paddle. I would've done the same. That's why our partnership has endured.

We'd barely traveled 30 feet from the little beach where we'd launched the canoe when my deer hair bass bug disappeared in an implosion of water. I lifted my rod and felt the hard pull of a strong fish.

Doc chuckled from the stern. "This might get boring."

"Never," I grunted. "I love big bass."

The fish never jumped, but it fought the bend of my 7-weight bass-bugging rod with hard circling runs, and it wasn't until I had it alongside the canoe that Doc started laughing.

"What's so funny?" I said.

"You got yourself a bluegill, there, bud."

"Can't be," I said.

But it was a bluegill, all right. A rather large bluegill, in fact.

"Nuts," I grumbled as I eased the barbless bass bug from its mouth and started to slide it back into the water.

"Hang on there," said Doc. "Take a look at that fish."

I couldn't get my hand around it. It was almost as big as a dinner plate. Its throat was brilliant orange, its belly golden, and its flanks glowed in subtle iridescent shades of olive-green and sky-blue. "It's gorgeous, isn't it," I said.

Doc nodded. "So what do you say?"

"Huh?" I said. "You wanna fish for bluegills?"

"Hell, yes. If that's a typical bluegill from this pond. . ."

"What about the bass?"

He waved away all thoughts of bass with the back of his hand. "Rig up that four-weight of yours, tie on a dry fly. This'll be great. Think about it. The bluegill's the perfect fish. It's pretty and strong, eats bugs off the surface, thrives just about everywhere, tastes terrific . . ."

"You've got to be kidding," I said.

Doc grinned. "Adjust your thinking, pal."

I was a mere toddler when I derricked the first fish of my life out of the water. It was, naturally, a bluegill. I can still see the sudden twitch and dart of the homemade wine-cork bobber, and I can hear my father, squatting beside me, whispering, "Wait . . . let him take it . . .

okay, now!" I yanked back on my rod, then came the circle-swimming tug and pull, and I yelled, "I got him! I got him!" before the little fish came skimming across the surface to me.

I still have the yellowing old black-and-white photograph to commemorate the day a bluegill hooked me on fishing, and it's probably that photo, rather than the specific memory, that makes the moment so clear to me after over half a century. I've watched a lot of cork bobbers twitch and dart since then, and I've crouched beside three toddlers of my own, whispering, "Wait . . . let him take it . . ."

In my family, anglers are initiated as soon as they can walk without falling down. A wine cork is split and bound to a leader and a worm is threaded onto a hook and lobbed out beside some lily pads. Then the rod—in my family, it's a fly rod—is handed to the child with the certain knowledge that it won't be long before a bluegill eats the worm and jiggles the bobber and creates a fisherman.

Bluegills occupy a special place in my angling heart, of course. But how can you take seriously the first fish you ever caught, and, a few years later, the first fish you caught on a fly? It's hard not to think of the bluegill as a kid's fish. Serious fishermen just naturally move on to more serious fish and leave the bluegills for the children.

These were the thoughts I had as Doc and I drifted on our little bass pond that July afternoon. "Adjust your thinking," he'd said, and as the afternoon slid into evening, and as we continued to catch big bluegills on trout-weight tackle, it became easier. They sipped dry flies, just like trout. They weren't sleek sprinters, and they didn't jump, but they were muscular street fighters, dogged and powerful.

No, they weren't all foot-long "pounders" like that first one, and yes, they were almost too easy to catch. They were neither selective nor wary, and we caught them until our arms ached.

As much fun as it was, I knew I would not give up trout and bass and salmon to devote the rest of my fishing life exclusively to bluegills. But something important happened to me that afternoon, something that I realized had been missing from my fishing life for too many years: I relaxed. I fished without self-imposed goals or expectations or pressures. I knew I would catch enough fish, and I knew I could make some mistakes without blowing the opportunity of the season.

Once in the late afternoon, Doc and I stopped casting for several minutes to watch a heron stalk the shallows and to admire the acrobatics of a kingfisher diving for fish, and it never occurred to us that we were wasting precious fishing time.

With their relatively small mouths and their customary diet (about 85 percent insects, 10 percent crustaceans, and 5 percent baitfish), bluegills are made for smallish flies and trout-weight gear.

On a good day, at a good pond, any toddler can catch a barrel of bluegills on worms or crickets or grubs. A well-twitched nymph will perform at least as well. Call me stubborn, call me a purist, but I rarely fish for bluegills with anything but a surface fly. When the water's flat under low-light conditions at dawn and dusk, and on any soft, overcast summer's day, I'll catch a barrelful myself. When conditions are poor I might only catch a few bucketfuls.

Bluegills are easy to lure to the surface. They cannot resist a fly with lots of wiggly, jiggly parts—buggy stuff like marabou, soft hackles, and rubber legs. Maybe it actually resembles something—an ant, a beetle, a damselfly, a spider—but a box of bedraggled old dry flies that you've retired from the trout wars will catch tons of bluegills for you, too. Cast toward shoreline cover—lily pads, overhanging bushes, fallen trees—or over a drop-off, and let it sit for a moment. Give it a twitch. Wait while its buggy parts quiver and the ripples die. Bluegills like to hover right under a fly, studying it, allowing themselves to be seduced before they lift their noses and suck it in.

Sometimes they slash like largemouths, leaving a hole in the water. More often, though, bluegills sip like trout. You'll hook almost all of them if you hesitate for a count of three before you set the hook with an easy strip strike.

Bluegills thrive in a wide range of water types, from cold and clear to warm and weedy, and they're found in all of the contiguous forty-eight states. You don't need fancy, high-powered watercraft to track them down. Low-tech transportation such as a canoe, a creaky old rowboat, or a float tube suits a low-tech fish like the bluegill. On a sultry summer afternoon, I find it refreshing to shuck off my shoes and socks, roll up my pantlegs, wade the shallows of my local millpond, and cast a bug along the weedy shoreline. Bluegills are generally scattered everywhere.

You can catch them year round, although bluegills are especially vulnerable during their spring spawning season, typically when the water temperature rises to about 67 degrees. They build their sandy saucer-shaped spawning beds in water 3 feet deep or less. The nests are easy to locate and logical targets for the angler. After the spawn, the male bluegills remain to guard the nests while the females, which generally run larger, lurk nearby in deeper water.

The world record bluegill was a 4-pound, 12-ounce monster taken in Alabama in 1950. In many waters, bluegills tend to run to a specific size, and 11- or 12-inch "pounders" like those Doc and I caught that day are certifiable lunkers. Where you consistently catch hand-sized (or smaller) bluegills, you are unlikely to find any much larger. A spot like Doc's and my secret pond, therefore, is a treasure, and worth keeping secret.

Bluegills reproduce as aggressively as they strike, and will, if unchecked by predators, outpopulate their food supply, so it's almost always a good idea to harvest them. Keeping a mess of bluegills is a good idea for another reason: Deep fried in beer batter, or rolled in cracker crumbs and sautéed in butter, bluegill filets are a gourmet's treat.

An afternoon of bluegill fishing almost forces you to blow out a long breath and smile. It's important therapy for any angler, and I have Doc to thank for reminding me. Now that I've adjusted my thinking, I've come to believe that he might be right: The bluegill could be the perfect fish.

Just Fishin' with Uncle Ray

I grew up in a *Field & Stream* family.
My father wrote his "Tap's Tips" and "Sportsman's Notebook" columns
for thirty-odd years for that magazine, and I fished and hunted with
Dad and his fellow columnists Ed Zern and Corey Ford—and others
who wrote for the magazine, like Lee Wulff, Harold Blaisdell, and
Burton L. Spiller. I got my monthly fix of African adventure from
Robert Ruark and angling instruction from Al McClane.

Those are my roots. I had a filial devotion to *Field & Stream*,
mainly because the demands of writing his monthly columns gave
Dad an unassailable excuse to spend lots of time outdoors, and he was
the kind of father who liked to bring his kid along. So the magazine
indirectly subsidized my education as a fisherman and bird hunter.

But like many kids of my generation, I devoured all the magazines.
We were not parochial in my house. The treasures arrived monthly—
Sports Afield and *Outdoor Life*, the other two members of the so-called
"Big Three," plus *Argosy*, *True*, *Esquire*, and *Sports Illustrated*, which
always had a lot of hunting and fishing stuff in them, too.

My father was . . . well, he was my father. I probably took him for granted, the way kids do. I guess I took Corey Ford and Ed Zern and Lee Wulff for granted, too. I saw them in their long johns, I lay awake in lakeside cabins listening to them snore, and I knew they sometimes got skunked, busted off fish, tied bad knots, and went in over their waders—important lessons for a boy. These men were good to me. They always treated me more or less as an equal. But I knew them too well to consider them heroes.

I never met Ray Bergman, but I felt as if I knew him, too. I didn't exactly think of him as a hero, either. He seemed way too down-to-earth and accessible. More like a favorite uncle. Probably because I never saw him in his long johns, he was my favorite outdoor writer of them all. When *Outdoor Life* arrived at our door, I grabbed it and went fishin' with Uncle Ray.

He wrote the way an uncle would talk to his favorite nephew—simply, gracefully, humbly, and wisely—and he didn't sneer at worm fishing, which was my specialty in those days, or look down his nose at bluegills, horned pout, and perch, which were my most available quarry.

Ray Bergman told stories, and he found lessons in every experience. He was scrupulous about getting the facts right, and he didn't exaggerate. "In relating these incidents," he wrote, "I have given only actual facts. There have been many times when the methods described . . . did not produce. These experiences, being failures, could not possibly contribute anything to angling knowledge unless the exact cause of failure were known and the experience related as a warning illustration. Fishermen are sometimes criticized for telling only of the times when certain lures produced. But usually such incidents are the only ones worth recounting. I simply don't want you to believe that I always succeed. My failures, like those of most anglers, are legion."

You could trust Uncle Ray.

"When I was a boy," recalled Ray Bergman, "conditions were quite different from what they are today. I am old enough to have experienced the old-fashioned ways of the latter part of the nineteenth century and the rapid-fire progress of the twentieth. I saw the horse and carriage give way to the automobile, the dusty roads change rapidly from macadam to Tarvia and then to concrete. Each advance of progress had its effect on the fishing."

Bergman was born in 1891 and grew up in rural Nyack, New York, on the banks of the Hudson River, and by the time he was twelve he'd become a fanatical fisherman. "Being so closely attuned to nature's whims," he wrote, "I drifted naturally into out-of-door pursuits, and fishing seemed to be the one sport which best gratified that innate craving for an intimacy with those forces of which I knew so little. Is it any wonder that I made the study of fishing my life's work?"

From the beginning, Bergman kept detailed notes of his fishing experiences. It was a habit that he continued throughout his life. Those records led him to understandings he would write about, and they gave him the stories and anecdotes that entertained his readers and illustrated his points. "Remember that in the following incidents," he wrote, "I am not trying to prove anything. They are simply accurate accounts of actual fishing experiences. If between them I wander into fanciful theory I hope the reader will forgive my mood, overlook it, and draw his own conclusions from the facts themselves."

He took note of every conceivable variable—weather and wind, time of day and year, phase of moon, condition of water, lures and baits that worked and failed, tactics and techniques, rods and reels, fish behavior and habits—and he was unique, at least for his time, in understanding that *all* of the variables needed to be factored into the complex angling equation.

Ray Bergman fished for everything that swam in his Hudson Valley waters—trout, bass, pickerel, pike, salmon, lake trout, walleyes, panfish, even carp and suckers—and he made understanding all of them his "life's work" long before he would ever get paid for it. He wrote with equal affection about all species of freshwater fish.

Bass he found to be, in their own way, as challenging as trout. "In trout fishing," he wrote, "practically all lines and methods of presenting them are designed with one objective in view: an appeal to the appetite of the fish. In fishing for bass we find that factors other than the desire for food must be considered." He especially loved fishing for bass with popping bugs. "Surface lure angling is to me the acme of fishing, as judged by the amount of enjoyment derived, and in fly rod surface fishing for bass I find the most delicate and refined expression of bass fishing."

Bergman fished with bait and plugs and spinners and spoons, but he always had a special fondness for fly fishing. "No one in our territory ever used flies," he recalled, "nor did they know anything about fly fishing. Even as recently as 1920, I doubt if there were more than six fly fishermen in our community. . . . I tried my best to get others interested in fly fishing but it was slow work."

When it was time to earn a living, he opened a sporting goods store—with a well-stocked fishing department—in his hometown of Nyack. Illness soon forced him to quit that business, and during his long recuperation, he began to write fishing articles. "I started writing," he recalled in 1959 in "Ray Bergman Says Goodbye," his last column for *Outdoor Life*, "simply because I loved fishing and wanted to share what I learned from my endless experiments with fishing tackle and tactics. Rather like a person airing his ideas through a letter to the editor, I typed out my first fishing story in 1921 and mailed it to the old *Forest and Stream* magazine. The story was published, and I have been writing similar stories ever since. All my writing has followed the same basic concept: to give the reader factual information gained and tested by my own practical experience, and to make it as interesting as my writing ability would allow."

He continued to write articles for the sporting magazines of the day for the next decade, and he published his first book in 1932. *Just Fishin'* was an instant classic and went through many editions. Unlike most comprehensive angling books of that time, *Just Fishin'* gave trout and bass equal space and revealed the fact that Bergman spent as much time fishing warm waters as he did wading trout streams. While he spurned no method that might catch fish, he often chose the fly rod when others in his party fished with bait or plugs, and he seemed to take special delight whenever his flies outfished their methods.

Ray Bergman's first fishing column for *Outdoor Life* appeared the next year, in 1933, and continued for twenty-six years, giving his readers more than three hundred visits with Uncle Ray. In between, he wrote two more classics: *Trout* (1938) and *Fresh Water Bass* (1942).

In July of 1967, just five months after Ray Bergman's death, my father received a letter from his friend Matthew Hodgson, who was then an editor at Houghton Mifflin. "I have just had a note from Angus Cameron," Hodgson wrote to Dad. "He seems interested in my idea of publishing an anthology of Ray Bergman's best [*Outdoor Life*] pieces, edited by yourself."

My father, an admirer of Bergman, was eager to do the project, but the publishers of *Field & Stream*, for whom Dad was at the time a columnist, would not permit one of their writers to associate his name with a project involving one of their Big Three rivals. So Dad recommended his friend Ted Janes for the project, and in 1970, *Fishing with Ray Bergman* was published.

Now, alas, all four Bergman books are out of print and hard to find. I treasure my copies. I dip into them often, and while technology has changed considerably since the days when Ray Bergman was writing, the fish—and the fishing—aren't much different. I still find his stories as wise and as entertaining as I did half a century ago when I was a kid waiting for *Outdoor Life* to arrive in my mailbox.

The Pig Boat

Spinning reels, bass boats, fish-finders, plastic baits, and other high-tech equipment arrived in Tom Nixon's part of Louisiana shortly after World War II, but he stuck to the fly rod. Not that he was a grumpy old traditionalist or any kind of fly-rod snob. "All I owned were a couple fly rods," he told me shortly before he died in 2003, "and I couldn't really afford new gear. Anyway, I'd always done okay with flies, and I can be pretty stubborn."

Nixon wanted to catch bass as much as the next guy, though, and he didn't like getting outfished by his high-tech friends. "I was having to put up with a lot of guff from some of my heave-and-crank acquaintances about fly-rod bass," he remembered, "how they should save their fish because the fly rod was unable to put anything into the pot. I will not bore you with all of the inconsiderate, meaningless and unjustified abuse that was heaped on my poor innocent head. But let me assure you, I was looking hard for something more productive to hang on my leader than the conventional fly baits of the time."

In 1951 Nixon responded to this challenge by inventing the Calcasieu Pig Boat, which was inspired by the Hawaiian Wiggler, a popular post-war, rubber-legged baitcasting lure. The Pig Boat resembled no "fly" anyone had ever seen. He named it after the Calcasieu River, his home bass water in southwestern Louisiana. The fly proved lethal on bass. Nixon likened it to a German submarine, which, he said, was "a deadly underwater predator" known during the Second World War as a "pig boat."

In fact, Tom Nixon's Pig Boat should properly be regarded as nothing less than a revolutionary creation, a transitional design that liberated fly-rod bass fishing from the limitations of surface fishing with bugs and made it a legitimate sport for all water types and conditions. "Far too many capable and dedicated fishermen had wedded their fly rods to the cork body popping bug," he wrote, "and when this combination failed to produce, they called it a day and went home."

The Pig Boat's most prominent feature—dozens of wiggly rubber legs entirely encircling the body—makes it more of a lure than a fly. It was the first bass "bait" specifically designed to be cast and fished with the fly rod. Its body resembles a Woolly Worm—heavy black chenille wound over with thickly palmered grizzly hackle. From 56 to 72 strands of thin, black, rubber thread are tied as a collar in front.

In your hand, a Pig Boat looks like a mating cluster of tarantulas. In the water, it wiggles and shimmies in ways that bass—and, in fact, most species of fish—cannot resist.

In 1954, Harold F. Blaisdell's *Field & Stream* story "Pig Boat on the Furnace" brought Nixon and his creation national attention. Blaisdell suspected that the Pig Boat would make an enticing mouthful for big predatory brown trout, and he proved it one evening on Furnace Brook, his local Vermont trout stream. "What puzzled me," recalled Nixon tongue-in-cheekly, "was why anyone would waste a good bass bait on brown trout. . . . Mr. Blaisdell received a good bass bait and promptly let some old brown trout slobber all over it."

The original black-and-grizzly Pig Boat worked great most of the time. But Nixon didn't stop there. Wrapping lead wire around the hook shank sank the fly down to water levels where bass sometimes lurked out of reach of an unweighted version. Clamping a spinner ahead of it added bass-attracting flash in murky water. Rigging it with an offset spinner converted the Pig Boat into a deadly fly-rod spinnerbait, while a 6-inch plastic worm split in half and trailed behind a Pig Boat made a lethal bass lure. When he discovered that impaling a pork rind on the hook sometimes caught more bass than an unfettered Pig Boat, Nixon tied in a sprig of white rubber threads as a pork-rind substitute and called it a "Sproat Boat."

He made them in different colors and sizes, and varied his retrieves according to weather and water conditions—deep and slow, fast and shallow, and even dead-drifted in lazy southern river currents.

The effectiveness of his Pig Boat encouraged Nixon to experiment by fly casting with spin-fishing bass baits such as plastic worms, jig-n-pigs, and spinnerbaits. And then he devised "flies" that worked as well. In the process, he showed the way for present-day, fly-rod-casting bass gurus who no longer restrict themselves to floating bugs and whose repertoire of skills, tactics, and lures rivals that of the tournament champions. "A bass," Nixon wrote, "is a far cry from the conventional target of the long rod. So, when the conventional concepts of tackle, lures and procedures fail to interest an unconventional quarry, go it his way."

Which is not to say that Tom Nixon ever turned up his nose at "conventional" flies. In fact, he invented dozens of more-or-less conventional flies and bugs and adapted countless old standards for southern largemouths and bream. All of them are proven fish-takers. He gave some of them delightful Cajun names—Sowela, Phideaux, Zeeke, Zombola, Maziere, Emida. Other names just seem to fit—Poofy, Big Sister, Shifty, Dog, Butcher.

My personal favorite Nixon fly name is the .56%er. It's a little weighted gray-and-yellow trout nymph that is also deadly for Cajun "brim"—and, same species, New England bluegills. Nixon observed that no trout dry-fly purist is really 100 percent pure. "A thorough analysis," he noted slyly, "shows 99.44 percent to be the maximum degree of purity attainable, but they are 100 percent fishermen. . . . This scrawny-looking misfit of a fly was offered and accepted because no one could possibly blame a guy for trying one out in the upstream riffle. It would be obvious to any passerby that the angler was just filling out the remaining .56 percent of his total fishing capacity and could not be seriously accused of fishing. And by that number the fly became known."

Twenty-five years ago, when a local bass club invited Tom Nixon to participate in their tournaments on the Toledo Bend Reservoir on the Texas-Louisiana border, he accepted the chance to stack his fly rod up against their spinning and baitcasting gear. He entered five tournaments. "Got one first, one second, and two thirds," he recalled. "The other one I got disqualified. We were camping out, and the alarm didn't go off. Slept through the start." He caught all of his tournament bass on two flies—most of them on a spinner-and-Pig-Boat rig ("for underwater") and some on a yellow cork-body popping bug ("when I found 'em on top").

Tom Nixon was never much for philosophizing. But his love of fly tying and fly fishing for bass bubbled forth from his conversation, and it still does from his writing. "The easy grace of a fly rod," he wrote in 1977, "the thrill it affords in playing and landing a fish, the casting accuracy that is accomplished, all of these things make the long rod one of the most sporting and pleasant ways to fish for bass."

PART IV

~~~~~~

SALT WATER

~~~~~~

To paraphrase Will Rogers, I never met a fish I did not like. But in the two main areas of my fly-fishing life—salt water and fresh water—there are distinct favorites. In fresh water it is trout. In the salt it is snook. None of the others comes close.

—Norm Zeigler, *Snook on a Fly*

I had never cast to a moving fish before, and the prospect of aiming flies at fast-swimming targets excited me. But my enthusiasm didn't last long. I soon found that I couldn't see a single fish—I might as well have been fishing at midnight. And even if I had been able to spot one of those invisible phantoms, I would not have known what to do next.

—Dick Brown, *Fly Fishing for Bonefish*

The only difference between big-game fishing and collecting old millstones is that millstones aren't slimy.
In between fishing expeditions, big-game fishermen go around lifting Percheron horses off the ground and pulling loaded freight cars with their teeth. In the evening, they gather in small groups and feel each other's muscle.
Big-game anglers and fresh-water anglers sneer at each other.
And why not?

—Ed Zern, *The Hell with Fishing*

First Light

One morning many Junes ago, before saltwater fly fishing became "the thing to do" in New England, Rip Cunningham, then the publisher and editor-in-chief of *Saltwater Sportsman* magazine, called me on the phone. "The stripers," he said without prologue, "are all over the place down here."

"I've been hearing stories," I said. "Figured it was a lot of exaggeration."

"The stories are true," said Rip. "They're back. It's really quite awesome. They're sloshing on the surface and cruising the mud flats at first light. You can see 'em pushing wakes in water barely up to your shins. Sometimes they tip up and wave their tails in the air. It's like bonefishing. We've been catching lots of them. It's all hunting and sight-fishing. Smallish flies, medium-weight rods. Stealth and cunning. Right up your alley. You've got to do this."

"What do you mean," I said, "by lots?"

"Well," he said, "my brother-in-law and I got about thirty between us in a couple hours this morning."

"Thirty in two hours," I repeated. Rip, I knew, did not exaggerate. I did the math. Fifteen fish per hour between the two of them. One striper every eight minutes per fisherman. That's about as fast as you can throw out a fly and haul in a strong fish. "That," I said, "*is* lots."

"Big ones, too," he said. "We landed three keepers, saw several others. Of course, we didn't actually keep 'em. They'll be back again tomorrow. Anyway, there are plenty of others. We saw, I don't know, hundreds of fish. But who knows how long it's gonna last? I haven't seen stripers like this for twenty-five years."

"Wait a minute," I said. "You said you got thirty *this morning*?" I looked at my watch. "It's still this morning."

"This isn't morning," Rip said. "Hell, it's—what?—almost ten-thirty. The sun's high in the sky. This is the middle of the day. Fishing's no good now. We quit hours ago."

"Okay, okay," I said. "You got me. Where and when?"

"Tomorrow at the Duxbury launch. Four o'clock."

"Four a.m. you mean."

"If we're on the water by four-fifteen," he said, "we'll hit it perfectly."

"Easy for you to say," I said. "You live there. Me, I've gotta drive two hours."

"I released one that measured forty-one inches," said Rip. "Dropped a little chartreuse-and-white bucktail in front of this shadowy wake and she just finned over to it and opened her mouth and sucked it in. About a foot of water. All hell broke loose. But, hey, if you'd rather sleep in ..."

"I'll be there," I said. "You know I will."

In those days I generally went to bed around midnight, read myself to sleep, and woke up around seven. But after dinner the night before my rendezvous with Rip, I loaded my gear into my car, set my alarm for 1:30, and went to bed. Naturally, I lay awake imagining myself casting to giant wakes in shallow water. I couldn't shake the feeling that if I let myself fall asleep, the alarm would fail to wake me up.

I stared into the darkness until around one in the morning. Then, I got up, put on the coffee, and fried myself some eggs and bacon. I left my house a little before two for the long drive-in-the-dark to Duxbury.

I found myself feeling quite virtuous about it, too. The houses and gas stations along the roadways were darkened, and I figured the occasional other vehicle I saw on the highway was headed home. They were at the end of something. Me, I was at the beginning. I had the jump on everybody.

When I got there, Rip was already messing around in his boat. He looked at his watch and said, "Let's get going." He made no mention of my virtue.

We rigged our rods by flashlight, and then Rip cranked up his outboard and maneuvered his boat among the black silhouettes of the sailboats and yachts that were moored in the harbor. A bell buoy clanged hollowly in the misty darkness. Gulls and cormorants perched on the pilings.

We cleared the harbor as the purple sky was beginning to fade to pewter, and we beached Rip's boat on a half-tide mud flat just as the first pale blush of pink appeared on the eastern horizon.

We stepped out of the boat. Rip pointed. "There," he whispered. "Let's go!"

It took a minute for my eyes to adjust. Then I saw them. Wakes. Swirls. Shadows. Here and there, a fin breaking the surface. Stripers, big ones, cruising the flats chasing bait and grubbing for worms and crabs.

In my youth I was a confirmed Night Person. I did my most creative and efficient work in the blackest hours after midnight. I went to bed late and slept late, and that didn't even count the parties.

As I grew older it changed. For a while, I was a Morning Person. Nothing ridiculous. Seven to noon saw me at my best, such as it was.

Now I don't know what you'd call me. A Daybreak Person, maybe. I want to be outdoors at first light, the magic hour before sunrise. I want to be there when it happens, and I'm willing to give up a night's sleep for it.

That morning many years ago with Rip Cunningham made me a convert. Oh, I still need a reasonable hope for good fishing. You can't talk me into getting up to meet a six o'clock tee time, or to go jogging, or to catch a commuter train.

But if you put a mug of black coffee in my hand and remind me of what it's like just when the sky fades from purple to gray and the stars begin to wink out and a thin mist blankets the water's surface, if you help me remember the way Bighorn brown trout sip Trico spinners on a late-August dawn, or how largemouth bass hump and slosh in weedy coves at first light in July, I'll be there. You won't have to ask me twice.

Fred Jennings guides for stripers in the tidal creeks that fill and drain the marshes along the Massachusetts north shore. He follows the tides in his canoe and catches striped bass on trout-weight rods. Fred has devised an algorithm for predicting how good the fishing will be, a complicated factoring of variables that include tide, sunrise, moon phase, season, wind direction, air and water temperatures, and a few mysterious unknowns that he doesn't share. He calls it the Estimated Fishing Quality Index—EFQI. As far as I can determine, the key variable is time of day, and the prime time of day is daybreak. What Fred calls "peak dawns" or "magic mornings" occur when the sun rises precisely three hours after the turn of the high tide.

He wants to be in his canoe an hour before that.

Fred's guide fee follows a sliding scale depending on the day's EFQI. I know of no other guide who does this, but it makes sense. He charges most for a peak dawn—a "platinum morning"—when tide and time line up perfectly. Supply and demand, explains Fred, who's an economist by trade. By his calculations, only twelve platinum mornings occur between May and October, one every two weeks, and those are the days that everybody who reads his EFQI charts wants to book.

I've left my house at 2 AM several times for a rendezvous with Fred Jennings to witness a peak dawn on his marsh. The water lies flat calm under a wispy blanket of mist, and feeding stripers leave wakes and swirls around the clam flats and against the mud banks. It is, truly, magical.

It stands to reason that fish are happier, less guarded, hungrier, and more aggressive at first light after the lulling comfort of darkness. Nighttime shelters them from their predators. Water temperatures cool down to their comfort zones. Insects and baitfish are slow and naïve and vulnerable in the early hours. Fish—saltwater and freshwater alike—are ready to go prowling in that marginal time between night and day.

But it's more than that. Fishermen are energized and predatory, too. Or at least this fisherman is.

Somehow the world feels a lot different—more alive, more optimistic—when I'm leaving for an outdoor rendezvous before dawn on a summer's morning than it does when I'm coming home at that time.

"The morning," said Thoreau, "which is the most memorable season of the day, is the awakening hour. Then there is least somnolence in us; and for an hour, at least, some part of us awakes which slumbers all the rest of the day and night."

Rip and I immediately got into fish in the gray half light. Then he stopped casting and whispered, "Lookit that." He pointed to the east.

I looked just in time to see, suddenly and all at once, the sun crack the line between ocean and sky. It was like turning on the lights. Day—literally—broke, and the night was abruptly and entirely gone, and I found myself smiling, because I was there, and you weren't.

Silence on the Flats

I was standing up on the casting platform of Captain Dexter Simmons's 18-foot *Flatsmaster*, 8-weight fly rod in my right hand and a size-2 Del Brown's Merkin pinched by the bend of the hook between the forefinger and thumb of my left. I was bent tensely forward at the waist, left foot ahead of right, rocking with the boat's movement as Captain Dex, my guide, who was perched high on his poling platform behind me, pushed us over the flats. We were nosing into both the soft wind and the outgoing tide. We expected the permit to be facing the same way we were moving, cruising the shallow water, looking to intercept any unfortunate crabs—including the odd size-2 Merkin—that might come bumping along the bottom to them. We hoped to sneak up behind them, spot them before they spotted us, and drop a fly in front of their unsuspecting noses.

The mid-day sun hung high and hot overhead. There wasn't another boat in sight. Nothing at all except us and a few pelicans. The empty flats stretched from horizon to horizon. The ocean was a great flat dinner plate washed in myriad shades of azure and aquamarine under the big bowl of a pale, cloudless January sky. I wore a short-sleeved shirt, quick-dry pants, billed cap, sunscreen. Snowbound New England was far behind me, and I was thrilled just to be there with a fly rod in my hand.

Key West in early January was a winter getaway for Vicki and me after a nasty New Hampshire December and, for that matter, a bad year in general. I had assumed the flats would be barren and had not expected to go fishing.

But Captain Dexter assured me that there were fish. The water temperatures had been favorable. He'd been seeing some bonefish. On New Year's Day a client caught a 7-pounder, in fact. There had been decent numbers of permit. And there were always barracuda and jacks and ladyfish and other fun species, if you weren't too snobby.

I told him I wasn't snobby at all, but permit were sure intriguing.

We talked in quiet voices for a while, getting acquainted—family, mutual friends, striped bass, permit flies, the relative merits of Sage, Winston, and Orvis rods—our eyes all the while scanning the water, looking for fish. Dex talked about tides and cold fronts, moon phases and barometric pressure, the way bait and bonefish and permit moved onto and off the Key West flats in the winter. I talked about New England trout streams and bass ponds. He'd grown up in Rhode Island, but that was a long time ago. He said he sometimes missed the winters.

Gradually we lapsed into silence. We were, after all, permit hunting, and it was a serious business that demanded our full attention. Even under ideal conditions, we wouldn't expect to see a lot of fish, and we knew that we wouldn't get many shots at those that we did manage to spot. Even if Dex saw them early, I cast quickly, and my shots were accurate, we understood that very few permit agreed to eat flies, no matter how well they were cast and how closely they resembled crabs.

Thomas McGuane wrote: "What is most emphatic in angling is made so by the long silences—the unproductive periods. For the ardent fisherman, progress is toward the kinds of fishing that are never productive in the sense of the blood riots of the hunting-and-fishing periodicals. Their illusions of continuous action evoke for him, finally, a condition of utter, mortuary boredom. . . . No form of fishing offers such elaborate silences as fly-fishing for permit."

We expected no "blood riots," but we did hope to spot some fish. That would get our own juices boiling. Meanwhile, we hunted in silence.

Captain Dexter's job was to move us across the flats and to locate the permit before they located us. My job was to see the fish, if not before Dex did, then certainly when he pointed them out to me, and then to make one good cast, close enough to the fish that it would see the fly, but not so close as to spook the ever-spooky permit. One good cast was all it would take. One cast is usually all you'd get.

I was obsessing about seeing, and about the frustration of looking without seeing, fighting the boredom of looking hard for a long time and seeing nothing. It had been over three years since I'd hunted for fish on the flats, and I'd left my permit eyes back in Belize. If my eyeballs were biceps, I'd've been flexing them, straining to see, looking hard through my polarized glasses to separate the surface ripples and the wavering turtle grass and the shimmering underwater shadows from the ghosty movements and undulating shapes of the permit that I desperately wanted to see.

Sometimes, I remembered, they just materialized there, with their black backs and sickle tails, conjured up by the sheer force of my imagination—because I wanted to see them, because I was afraid of missing them, because I believed that if I looked hard enough for long enough my diligence would surely be rewarded.

Mostly, those fish I saw were illusions, and I had learned not to mention them. The flats are densely populated with illusions.

And then suddenly Captain Dexter broke our long silence.

"Okay, we got permit," he whispered. "Eleven o'clock. Eighty yards. Moving right. Two—no, three fish. Nice ones."

And I flexed my eyeballs, and . . . no, I saw nothing but turtle grass and ripples.

"I don't see 'em." I could hear the desperation in my voice. "Where—?"

"One o'clock now," said Captain Dex, his voice surprisingly calm. I'd heard the stories about the Key West guides, how they yelled and cursed and sulked when their clients screwed up. But Dex wasn't like that. "Look, there," he said, and he pointed with his pole. "Seventy-five feet now, turning this way. See 'em?"

Yes! "Okay," I said. "Got 'em!" Suddenly they were obvious, and once I saw them, I couldn't understand how I'd ever failed to see them, and I locked on them, those shimmering shapes, those elusive shadows that I knew I'd lose if I looked away for just an instant.

Spotting those permit and finding myself within fly-casting distance of them seemed, all by itself, like a triumph. We'd been out there on the flats for well over an hour, straining our eyeballs under the high January sun in that long silence. Now we had fish.

Dex pivoted the boat subtly, putting the three permit at eleven o'clock so that he would not be in line with my backcast. The fish were poking along close to the bottom, more or less side-by-side, moving slowly. Looking for bait, I thought. Happy, hungry fish. Fish that might be willing to eat a well-cast size-2 Del's Merkin.

I had told Dex—it came out as a kind of confession—that I'd never actually caught a permit. I'd hunted them several times from the casting platform of a flats boat. I'd had shots at permit. I'd messed up some of them, spooking the fish. Mostly, they'd simply ignored my flies, or had failed to locate them. But I'd seen fish turn on my fly, too, and once, in Belize three years earlier, on a gray morning on a half tide near the shoreline of a mangrove cay—every detail of that encounter remains vivid—a permit ate my crab fly, and I'd felt the power of his round body as he sliced across the flats, headed for the reef. I'd managed to turn him short of the coral head that surely would've cut my leader, and I'd bullied him close to the boat, and he was silvering on his side, beaten, barely waving his tired tail, when he came unbuttoned, and my line went slack, and he slowly righted himself and swam away.

It was a terrible story, and I hated to tell it, but it was my only permit story, and its punchline was: "Bad knot."

The permit were 60 feet away now, coming straight at us.

"Now," whispered Dex.

I rolled out a cast, let the line pull the Merkin from my fingers, one hard backcast, a mistimed haul on the forecast, and my line and weighted crab fly flopped out there . . . 20 feet short, knocked down by the breeze and my own buck fever.

"Again," said Dex, and I heard no exasperation whatsoever in his voice.

I took in line, lifted, double-hauled, and the line rolled out, cutting through the wind in a tight loop.

"Yes," hissed Dex. "Good. Wait . . . now strip."

When I reached to strip, I saw that the running line had come up against my stripping guide in a knotty tangle. I tucked my rod into my armpit and picked desperately at the coil. If a permit took my fly now, he'd either break off or that knotted line would rip the guides off Dex's rod.

"Strip," repeated Dex, and this time I heard something in his voice. "He's looking at it. Come on. *Strip!*"

I tugged again at the knot, got it loose, gripped the rod, stripped.

"Nope," said Dex. "Too late. He gave it a look, then turned away."

"Oh, man," I said. "That was a good shot. I'm sorry. If my line hadn't gotten tangled . . ."

"Hey," he said. "They're permit. He probably wouldn't've eaten it anyway. They usually don't. Let's go find another one."

We hunted until the tide flattened out, and we saw several more permit, got a couple of decent shots, no bad screw-ups, but no takers, either, no blood riots. Mostly, we drifted across the vast empty flats in long comfortable silences, just happy to be there.

Turkey Bones

When Keith called from Maine, I figured it meant he had stripers on his mind.

What he said was: "Tomorrow."

"The boat landing?"

"Four o'clock."

"AM or PM?" I said, the only response that might forestall a hangup.

"PM."

"That's a relief."

"Tide," he elaborated, and hung up.

Keith had already untrailered and loaded his camouflaged duck boat at the landing when I got there. I grabbed my gear from the back seat and went down to the water's edge. I frowned and pretended to look around. "Where's the damn boat?"

It was our old joke, and he grinned quickly, then jerked his head at the 9-weight fly rod I was carrying. "I see you brung your toy rod."

Another of our old jokes, which he thought was funnier than I did.

"I can land a keeper on this," I said.

"Well, suh," he said, "I surely do hope you can. Course, you've gotta hook one, first."

Keith and I climbed into his duck boat, and he steered it through the marsh and up a meandering tidal creek. We made jokes about being invisible, and we reminisced about how the 5-horse Johnson motor had never failed us, well, except for that one time a few Decembers ago when we were hunting eiders out on the bay and the ice storm came in.

"She's totally dependable in good weather," Keith said. "Like some fishing partners I know."

Finally, unable to restrain myself any longer, I said, "So you found a hot spot, huh?"

"Ayuh."

"Big ones?"

"Mebbe."

"Keepers?"

Apparently exhausted from all that conversation, he just shrugged, which I took for an affirmative.

We followed the creek through a couple miles of marsh before Keith turned the boat around and cut the motor to trolling speed. He pointed at the shoreline, where the outgoing tide swirled around rocks and cut deep holes against the marsh grass. I began casting a chartreuse Deceiver, my most reliable striper fly.

I was vaguely aware that Keith had heaved something off the stern with his spinning rod and was dragging it behind us. A moment later he grunted. I turned. His rod was bowed. When he cranked the fish in, I saw that it was a large bass. He measured it against some markings on the boat, shrugged, and released it.

"How big?" I said.

"Thirty-three and change."

"Almost a keeper," I said. "I never caught a keeper. That's my goal. A thirty-six-inch bass. I don't want to keep it. I just want to catch one."

He shrugged. "Toy rod," he said.

We fished for an hour, during which time Keith caught five bass. None was quite a keeper, but all were within a few inches on either side of thirty. I changed flies a dozen times and never had a strike. Finally I said, "Lemme see what you're using."

A stiff wire leader was threaded through a 1-foot length of orange rubber tubing with a sand worm impaled on the hook at the end of the rig. He let it drag beside the boat. It looked like a snake undulating in the water.

"What in hell do you call that?" I said.

"Turkey bone. Wanna try?"

"No, thanks."

"Hang one on your fly rod."

"That's not fly fishing."

"Nope-suh," he said, "it definitely ain't. I promise not to tell."

"Thanks just the same," I said.

We chugged up and down the creek for another hour. I continued to get no strikes and Keith landed three more and lost a couple.

"Listen," I said. "Maybe I will try one of those turkey bones."

"On your toy rod?"

"No. Gimme that other spinning rod."

"You?"

"Sure. I'm not proud."

"Course not."

"You said you wouldn't tell."

So I trolled turkey bones from a spinning rod and began to catch stripers, and then I hooked one that felt bigger and stronger than the others. "Keeper," I grunted. "Gotta be." I cranked the handle of the spinning reel one way and the line kept moving the other way, and I tightened the drag and still that big striper took line, and I couldn't get leverage with the short spinning rod to turn the fish the way I could have with my 9-weight fly rod.

Once the striper rolled near the surface and we saw its breadth.

"Oh, my," whispered Keith.

Then it wrapped a piling and was gone.

We continued to troll turkey bones and caught a few more before the tide turned. All nice ones, but no keepers. We chugged silently back toward the landing as darkness gathered over the marsh.

Finally Keith said, "Somethin' wrong?"

I shook my head.

"You're unnaturally quiet."

"I'm thinkin'," I mumbled.

"I get it," he chuckled. "You finally seen the light. Gonna give up that toy rod and go after stripers with real gear, huh?"

"Nope-suh," I said. "Just tryin' to figure how I can tie a turkey bone fly."

The Bones of Deadman's Cay

Columbus dropped anchor at Long Island in the Bahamas in 1492 and named it "Ferdinanda" after his patron back in Spain. It was his third stop in the New World, right after San Salvador and Rum Cay.

Carolina loyalists fled to the skinny sliver of land (60 x 4 miles) and settled there with their slaves during the American Revolution. Their descendants live there still, mingling and intermarrying happily, fishing and growing bananas and diving for *langouste*, the local lobster with the insignificant front claws, and living the good island life.

It wasn't until 1996 that Garry King, a footloose fly fisherman from Bozeman, Montana, got wind of hundreds of square miles of sheltered, virgin bonefish flats halfway down the west coast of Long Island at Deadman's Cay. He went, he fished, and he ended up staying a month. "The bonefish," he reported, "had never seen a fly, and they were more plentiful than in any other area I had fished in the Bahamas." The fish averaged 5 pounds, and according to King, even a modestly skilled angler could reasonably expect to catch a dozen or so bones on an average day.

Within a year, King had helped his Bahamian friends Samuel Knowles and Wade Smith set up a little Mom 'n' Pop bonefishing operation at Deadman's Cay. Sammy, a crackerjack bonefisherman (he's won several Bahamas fly-fishing tournaments), was the guide. King, who's met them all, calls Sammy "the best bonefish guide in the Bahamas." Wade, a former pit boss in a Freeport casino, handled the accommodations. At first Sammy and Wade hosted just two fishermen at a time. They didn't spend a penny on advertising (they still don't), but King helped spread the word through the fly-fishing network. Within two years, Sammy had brought in his cousin Frank Cartwright and Frank's son, Jerry, as guides, and Wade had built a lodge that would sleep six anglers.

A few years ago my fishing buddies spent a week at Deadman's Cay without me. Never mind why I didn't go. As it turned out, my priorities were severely screwed up, and my so-called friends wouldn't let me forget it. When they got back, they tortured me with photos and stories—eagle-eyed guides, double-digit bonefish days, endless miles of unspoiled flats where they never saw another boat, thousands of happy tailing bones ranging up to 6 pounds that ate anything that dropped in front of them.

They wanted to go back. No way they'd leave me behind this time.

The first week of March, two years later. Back in New England our wives were bracing for what the wizards of weather were calling the Storm of the Century, and so what if the century was only a few years old.

Meanwhile, on a hard-bottomed, mangrove-rimmed flat a ten-minute boat ride from the landing at Deadman's Cay, Jerry, our guide, and Andy and I were creeping along in ankle-deep, 78-degree water. Jerry stuck close to my left shoulder. He had shrewdly sized us up and decided that Andy could manage on his own. I'd spent our first morning not seeing what Jerry and Andy were seeing.

Then: "Bones. Eleven o'clock."

Jerry pointed, and I looked, but my bonefish eyes were still somewhere back in Belize where I'd left them a few years ago. I felt like that blind golfer whose caddy sets his clubface behind the ball, lines up his feet, adjusts his shoulders, and tells him which way the wind's blowing and how far he has to hit it. "I don't see 'em, dammit," I said.

"Coming at you, man. Forty feet. Two of 'em. No. Three. They're turning left. Ten o'clock, now. See 'em?"

"No, I don't. Shit!"

Spotting bonefish is the whole point of fishing for them. But I'd forgotten what I was supposed to be looking for. Shadows and ripples and turtle grass and the high shimmering Bahamian sun created a thousand bonefish out there at ten o'clock.

Screw it. I made a cast. Was that 40 feet? Was that ten o'clock?

"Queek. Thirty feet. Nine-thirty now, moving to the left. Comin' fast. Cast again."

I did.

"Yeah, good shot. He turned. He's on it, man. *Streep.* Slow. Stop. Okay, now *streep* . . ."

I held my breath. Beside me, so did Jerry.

Then he let it out. "He looked at it. Didn't want it. Spooky damn bones. Cold front comin', that's why. The bones, man, they can feel it."

A few minutes and 40 yards later, Jerry again said, "We got bones." I thought I detected a note of resignation in his voice.

He pointed, and this time, *mirable dictu*, I saw them, shadowy shapes ghosting toward us, and I couldn't understand why I hadn't been seeing them all day. It was a little patrol, eight or ten reconnoitering bonefish, at two o'clock.

"Got 'em," I said.

I dropped my fly 5 or 6 feet in front of them, let it sink, gave it a twitch, stopped, stripped again . . . and I saw one of the shadows turn, and then I felt the tug. I stripped, came up on him, lifted my rod, and he was off on that first, unforgettable bonefish sprint, my first of the day, my first in several years, a sizzling, panicky dash for deep water. I held my rod high and watched the line zing through my guides.

Oh, yes.

Then my rod went limp.

Jerry laughed, then began sloshing across the flat where my fly line, now disconnected from my backing, was slithering away. Another in a lifetime of memorable knots.

When I caught up to Jerry, he was holding my line. "You still got your fish," he said. "He stopped running when he stopped feeling the pressure."

Jerry handed me the line, and I hauled it in hand over hand and landed, if that's the word for it, a 3-pound bonefish.

Off to my left, Andy was laughing and snapping pictures. "Behold the famous angling writer," he said.

"I'm gonna step on that camera," I said.

"Blackmail," said Andy. "Gotcha."

An hour later, we lost our sunlight. "The lights went out," observed Jerry. "Here comes the front. Look."

From the west, an immense black cloud was sweeping across the sky toward us like big blanket being pulled over our heads.

"Going for the boat," Jerry said.

"Rain?" I said.

"Don't mind rain, man." He made exploding motions with his hands. "Don't like lightning."

By the time Jerry returned with the boat, the rain was coming in torrents and the temperature had dropped about 10 degrees. It was, he said, the first rain they'd had in a couple of months.

It passed over in less than an hour. Behind it came a sharp westerly wind and a brittle sun. We huddled in our windbreakers and shivered.

"Not good, man," said Jerry prophetically.

I am known among my fishing companions as "KOD." Kiss of Death. Plan a trip with me and something is sure to go seriously wrong. If you believe my friends, in '96 I single-handedly flooded the Yellowstone River over its banks and destroyed our beloved Paradise Valley spring creeks. It was I who summoned a September blizzard upon the Bow River, a torrential rainstorm upon the Beaverkill, and a week of unseasonable gale-force winds—always the winds—on both of our trips to Belize.

That night at the poker table in Deadman's Cay when they started in on me, I reminded them of what was happening back home. We'd all talked to our wives. They were buried under 2 feet of wet snow, and it was still coming down. Predictions called for another day of it. They'd declared a state of emergency in Massachusetts.

"And here we are, boys," I said. "Playing poker on a screened porch, eating Bahamian bananas and sipping margaritas, wearing shorts and T-shirts. How bad is this?"

"Very bad," said Andy.

"I'm actually kinda chilly," said Randy.

"Sammy says it's gonna drive the bones off the flats," said Elliot. "He says they've never had a cold front come through this late in the season." He pointed his finger at me.

"You shoulda been here two years ago," said Steven.

"No way," said Jon. "If ol' KOD was here then, we would've had a tsunami."

I suggested that we should all take a few minutes to feel guilty about leaving our families to contend with New England's Storm of the Century, but they weren't buying it.

The airstrip on Deadman's Cay is a little more than an hour's flight in a prop-driven nine-seater from Nassau. From the air, the west coast of Long Island is a jumble of little mangrove islands and spits and peninsulas that create dozens of intimate lagoons and flats and backwaters. A long arm of land curls protectively around the entire area, sheltering it from the westerly winds as the mainland does from the easterlies. Even from 8,000 feet, you expect to see schools of bonefish gliding over the white sand and flashing their tails in the sun.

From a flats boat, you quickly get disoriented. You're into the labyrinth barely five minutes from the dock outside the lodge, and all hints of civilization disappear. Some entire days passed without our ever glimpsing the other two boats that we knew had to be nearby. Each of the guides seemed to have his secret flats. Some were roundish and man-made, left behind by a now-defunct salt-making operation. Others were long and skinny, like four or five football fields laid end to end. The shallow flats we prowled on foot, working with the wind to intercept the bones coming toward us. Deeper ones we fished from the boat deck while the guides poled.

Then there were the "outside" flats, vast stretches of sand-bottomed water—ankle-deep at low tide, knee-deep at high—that extended from horizon to horizon on the ocean side to the west. You could spend an entire morning walking one of them. Deep, turquoise channels separated them. As we discovered, giant schools of upward of two thousand bonefish prowled these flats. One morning, Steven and Randy, taking turns casting from the deck, boated 31 bones between them in a few hours on an outside flat.

Sammy estimates that they have 250 square miles of prime bonefish flats at Deadman's Cay. Recently, he says, anglers guided by other Long Island outfitters have begun to find their way onto their flats. No longer is the area virgin the way it was when Garry King explored it in 1996. Still, in a week, I never saw another boat other than one of our own plus an occasional native lobsterman.

Deadman's Cay is bound to be "discovered." Wade philosophically guesses that they've still got a few years of unsurpassed bonefishing before the crowds find it.

That Monday cold front dropped the water temperature on the inside flats a crucial few degrees, and for a couple of days, the bonefish were hard to find and harder to fool.

The barracudas and sharks, on the other hand, which typically express baleful indifference to a streamer dragged past their noses, seemed to have been activated by the cooler water. Throw a long skinny fly—preferably something chartreuse—toward a 'cuda and strip as fast as you can. If he so much as twitches, you've got his interest. Cast again. Strip. Faster!

You've got to drop a big, colorful streamer (red and white is a good combination) within a foot of a shark's snout. He's got poor eyesight, so move it fast to catch his attention. If he turns and follows, slow it down.

We hooked several 4-foot 'cudas and 60-pound lemon sharks when the bonefishing was slow. We boated none of them for a variety of reasons that all amounted to excuses. I never did ask the guides what they'd do if they had to bring a shark aboard, but I recalled how Hemingway shot himself in the leg with his .45 when he boated a shark. Enticing them to follow a fly, seeing the predatory ferocity of their take, feeling their power on the end of my line . . . that was enough, thank you.

Each day by degrees the wind abated and shifted out of the west. The air and the water began to warm up, and the bones started showing up on the outside flats. We followed squadrons of ten to twenty fish that we found patrolling the edges of the rocky outer islands, and on a few occasions we encountered battalions of a thousand or more milling around in knee-deep water. One morning Steven and I took turns plucking bonefish from a vast school while a dozen big lemon sharks circled our boat. Neither of us had any inclination to get out and wade.

Frank had us cut back to 20-pound tippet and crank down our drags so we could horse the bones in before the sharks nailed them.

We didn't always manage it. I still have visions of the shark that loomed up behind a bonefish I was about to land. He spread his jaws and showed me his teeth before he engulfed the panicky 20-inch fish on the end of my line. Ah, Quint.

In the best of circumstances, no matter where you are, bonefishing varies from day to day. Moon, tide, wind, barometric pressure, air and water temperature . . . variables both subtle and blatant affect where they are and how eager they are to bite. A cold front is the worst. Still, six days on the flats at Deadman's Cay convinced me that the place fairly swarms with bonefish. We saw thousands of them, including a few 10-pounders. And in the end, despite the lingering effects of that nasty cold front, we caught enough of them to cure any New Englander's cabin fever—especially when the folks back home were digging out from the Storm of the Century.

Well, the boys insisted it wasn't what it had been two years earlier. We didn't see many tailing bones. The fish were spooky and cautious. A matter of degree, I guess. It was still the best bonefishing I've ever had. If that makes me the KOD, I can live with it.

Spring Break

After Andy and I made our plans back in early January, my non-angling friends kept giving me nudges in the ribs and making lame dirty-old-man cracks. Spring break in Florida, eh? Bikinis, wet T-shirts, keg parties, limbo contests? Heh-heh.

I just smiled and said, "Snook."

My friends who don't fish thought "snook" was a funny word, especially when I pronounced it the old-fashioned way—"Snuke." A tactic for seduction, maybe? Or a drinking game? When I explained that it was a species of fish, they rolled their eyes and said, "A fish. I should have known."

Teaching at the university, I take my fishing trips when I can get them. I'm not complaining. May through August, my summer break, extends through our long trout/striper/largemouth bass New England summer.

Spring break happens at my school, as it does in just about every American college and university, during the first or second week in March, which is actually still winter, two or three weeks before the Vernal Equinox, so that's when my tolerant—and more flexible—fishing partner takes his break, too. We head south, of course. Last year Andy and I went to Patagonia. Before that it was the Bahamas, and Belize before that.

We're not complaining, but early March is not the ideal time to fish anywhere on the planet that we have yet found. It's almost autumn in southern Argentina. It gets cold, and the big winds howl, and the good hatches are mostly finished. The first week in March can be iffy for Bahamas bonefish and for tarpon and permit in Belize. Cold fronts and hard winds drive them off the flats.

If bad weather can happen during our angling spring breaks, we've learned, it will, whether the locals tell us it's commonplace or unusual, and we've come to expect it. Even so, how bad can it be when you're fleeing from a New England winter?

So this year Andy and I decided to target snook on the Gulf coast of Florida. Sanibel Island, to be exact, and for three good reasons: One, our friend Norm Zeigler, a certified snook guru, lives there; two, Sanibel bills itself as the Fishing Capital of the World; and three, neither Andy nor I had ever caught a snook.

Andy hooked one on a plug in the Panama Canal when he was in college more than a quarter of a century ago. That was the sum of our combined snook experience.

I've learned to take Chamber of Commerce claims with a grain or two of salt (Roscoe, New York, calls itself "Trout Town USA," and Norfork, Arkansas, is the "Home of the World Record Brown Trout"), but the fact that the marketing experts choose to focus their PR slogans on fishing in the first place has to mean something.

I don't take Norm with any amount of salt. We've been friends for close to fifteen years, and all that time he's been beseeching, bribing, begging, and blackmailing me to go down there so he can take me snook fishing. His e-mails over the years have had me drooling. And now he's written *Snook on a Fly*, the definitive (and only, as far as I know) book devoted entirely to fly fishing for this intriguing fish.

When I was a kid I devoured the general-interest hook-and-bullet magazines—*Field & Stream, Outdoor Life, Sports Afield*—and read as many fishing books as I could get a hold of. I wanted to do it all, of course, but four exotic (to me) species of gamefish snagged my imagination and haunted my dreams: Atlantic salmon, striped bass, tarpon, and snook.

The stripers eventually returned to the New England coast, and they have turned out to be the perfect fly-rod fish—better even than I ever imagined. I traveled far and fished hard and long before I managed to catch a couple of tarpon and a salmon.

But I still had never caught a snook. Never fished for snook. Never even seen a snook in person. Everything I knew about snook fishing came from reading—all those magazine articles, especially the homespun tales about casting plugs and flies against mangroves deep in the Everglades that the late, great Charley Waterman used to write for the back page of *Saltwater Sportsman*, the how-to chapters in some books, and the destination chapters in others, and, of course, Norm's relentless e-mails from Sanibel, and now his book.

I've done enough fishing to know that until you've actually done it, you don't know anything. But everything I'd read and heard convinced me that snook are terrific fly-rod fish. They embody those apparently contradictory fish qualities that I find endlessly intriguing, wariness and selectivity combined with aggressiveness and size and power, and they hang out in the kinds of places I love to fish—on mangrove-lined shorelines where casting to targets is like bass-bug fishing for largemouths, and along sand beaches where you can hunt and stalk them like bonefish.

But information is not understanding. I didn't *know* anything about fly fishing for snook. The time to find out was long overdue.

There are two kinds of fishing adventures (as identified by Winnie the Pooh and further defined by my father): *Ex*-plores and Expotitions.

Ex-plores are spontaneous, close-to-home forays to intriguing, previously unexplored places that you've noticed while driving the back roads or spotted on a topographic map or heard about from a guy in the hardware store, where you never know what you might catch, and where the possibility of catching nothing is part of the appeal. *Ex*-plores are undertaken with an open mind. Sometimes you discover something worth keeping secret. More often than not, they don't amount to anything except . . . an exploration, and that's always fun.

Expotitions, on the other hand, are scrupulously researched, intricately planned, deliciously complicated, and generally expensive journeys to faraway and exotic destinations where the fishing promises to be special, and where poor fishing, regardless of how you rationalize it—no matter how much wildlife you see, how much fresh air and sunshine you absorb, how many interesting new people you meet, and what fascinating new culture you experience—is a distinct disappointment.

The spring-break trips Andy and I take are full-blown Expotitions. Part of the fun is planning them—talking long-distance to local experts, reading all the books and articles and web pages we can find, arranging the lodging and guiding, reserving the airline seats and rental cars, researching and tying every conceivably useful fly we might want to try, assembling and packing the gear, daydreaming and anticipating.

We left Andy's house for the airport at 5:30 AM in the middle of a New England nor'easter, on the second day of March, for our snook Expotition to Sanibel Island. Freezing rain was falling on a foot of new snow and frozen old slush. The roads were treacherous. We almost missed our flight.

Seven hours later we stepped out of the Fort Myers airport into 85-degree sunshine and softly swaying palm trees.

It's always a magic carpet ride.

The cold front came swooping down that night. The next morning the thermometer read 62 degrees, and a brittle wind was blowing from the north, gusting 15 to 20 mph. Two days later a second cold front settled on top of the first, and the nighttime temperatures plummeted into the low 50s. Andy and I kept telling ourselves that these would be pleasantly balmy early-March days if we were back in New England.

But this was Florida, and the snook weren't happy. "They want warm water," Norm said. "This cold drives 'em off the flats and beaches and back under the mangroves."

One day, guide Steve Bailey poled us up some creeks and through some cuts deep into the jungle, and we threw snook flies against the mangroves. Now and then a shadowy shape slid out from under the bushes and trailed our flies. We tried speeding them up, slowing them down, twitching-and-pausing, tug-tug-tug. We changed flies—Norm's usually magical Schminnows, Sea-Ducers, Deceivers, and Clousers in colors ranging from white to chartreuse to brown and in sizes ranging from small to big. We even tried Gurglers. No hits.

"Lockjaw," was Steve's diagnosis. "Too cold."

We walked some beaches on the incoming tide, sight-fishing, and we spotted a few skittish snook. A couple of follows. No hits.

We haunted one of Norm's favorite snook hunting grounds— the Ding Darling National Wildlife Refuge, where the lagoons empty and fill on the tides and the culverts are snook magnets. We tried it in the morning and evening and mid-day, on the incoming and outgoing and flat tides. We saw a few cruising snook, heard others popping from somewhere out of sight. Once toward dark I hooked one, a strong sudden fish that jumped twice before coming unbuttoned. "Mouths like tarpon," said Norm. "You gotta hit 'em two or three times with a hard strip strike."

Okay, sure, I thought. *Next time.*

On our last morning in Florida, with two hours to fish before we had to pack up and head for the airport, the breeze was soft and the sun was hot, and we found snook in the wash along the beach. They came in singles, pairs, and packs of eight or ten, sometimes so close we could touch them with our rod tips. Andy landed two and broke off another. I landed none but had a satisfying number of follows and nips and a couple of brief hookups.

We debated bagging our flight. It was tempting. But in the end, duty called, and we turned our back on it and went home.

When I pulled into my driveway in New Hampshire that night, the thermometer read 3 degrees above zero.

The Hunt for November Reds

Charles Poindexter and I rendezvoused with guide Ben Floyd at the Isle of Palms Marina at 10 AM on the Thursday before Thanksgiving. We sat on the veranda sipping coffee and gnawing jerky and watching the moored boats and the brown pelicans bob on the choppy gray water. The rain was coming sideways on a hard southeast wind. The flapping of the flags sounded like musket shots.

According to our plan, this was to be the day I caught the first redfish of my life. I'd been looking forward to it for a long time.

"We haven't had rain in a month," Charles grumbled. "Day after day, calm, warm, sunny. T-shirts and sunscreen, sight-fishing for schooled-up reds. A typical Carolina autumn." He narrowed his eyes at me. "So today *you* show up, and—" he flapped his hand at the storm-tossed harbor "—tornado warnings, according to the weather channel."

"Go ahead," I said. "Blame me. I am known far and wide as the Kiss of Death. I am uncanny. You want to wreck some perfectly good fishing, just invite me along. Florida, Labrador, Belize, Alaska, Patagonia. You can't escape me. Everywhere I go, I bring my wait-till-tomorrow New England weather with me. Now we can add South Carolina to the list." I turned to Ben. "What do you think, Captain?"

He was squinting up at the sky. The clouds were dark and roiling. "If you think you can hit the water with a fly," he said, "I believe I can find us some redfish. Looks to me like this weather's going to pass over. Let's give it another few minutes."

"What about the, um, tornadoes?"

"No guts, no glory," he said, which I did not find entirely comforting.

Fifteen or twenty minutes later the rain stopped. Ben studied the sky, then stood up. "Let's go."

The three of us pulled on foul-weather gear and piled into Ben's 17-foot Maverick flats boat, and he steered us out of the harbor and through a maze of channels and estuaries and barrier islands. We passed under a highway bridge, and pretty soon we found ourselves in a bay surrounded by a vast expanse of marshland. We were, I knew, within a few double-hauls of downtown Charleston, but we could have been in the heart of the Everglades.

Ben cut the motor and climbed up onto his poling platform. "Somebody grab a rod," he said.

I looked at Charles. He waved his hand at me. "I'm not that good with a fly rod. In this wind I'd just embarrass myself."

"I don't mind embarrassing myself," I said. I selected a 7-weight and stepped up onto the casting deck.

Ben poled along the edge of the marsh, then turned up a little tidal creek. It soon narrowed until it was barely 12 feet wide. Here the tall grass gave us a little shelter from the wind. I figured if I cast sidearm and kept my backcast low—just over the top of the grass—I might be able to hit the water.

We watched for wakes and swirls and nervous water, but we saw nothing to cast to. Ben paused at some bends and cuts and openings where I tried a few blind casts. I managed to keep my fly in the water but caught nothing.

After a while we found ourselves at the entrance to a pothole where three smaller creeks converged. It was about the size of the floor of my barn back in New Hampshire. I could cover it all from where we were stopped.

Ben jammed his pole into the mud and tied it off. "This is the place," he said. "One of my secret redfish holes. We got ourselves a nice falling tide. Let's get serious. Tie this on."

He handed Charles a fly, and Charles gave it to me. It was a new one to me. It was tied on a long-shanked, curved, size-4 saltwater streamer hook. Its tail was as long as the hook and made from a mixture of black bucktail and black Flashabou. The body was closely packed black Krystal Chenille trimmed flat on the top and bottom and rounded on the sides in the shape of a long, skinny spoon.

"It's called a Wiggler," said Ben. "Local favorite. Let it sink and hop it back along the bottom. Long, slow strip, pause for it to sink, strip again. Reds'll mostly take it on the drop. You'll just see the leader twitch, so pay attention. With the hook bent like that, it's supposed to ride upside down."

"What's it imitate?" I said.

"Shrimp? Finger mullet?" He shrugged. "Ask the fish."

"I certainly will, if I can find one willing to talk to me."

I raked Ben's secret redfish hole with his black Wiggler. I hit the deep cut along the left side, the edges of the oyster island, the places where each of the three creeks emptied. Once, a gust of wind caught a sloppy cast and blew the fly into the grass. I said something unprintable. Charles said, "Tornado."

I changed to an orange Wiggler, then a chartreuse Wiggler, then a crab fly. I retrieved it faster, slower. I used quick hops and long steady pulls, and all I hooked were a few clusters of oysters.

Now and then a shrimp hopped out of the water, or a baitfish splashed. A few times something on the bottom sent a swirl to the surface. Clearly, there was life in this pothole.

But nothing ate my fly.

"What'm I doing wrong?" I said.

"Nothing," said Ben. "You're doing fine. I know there's redfish here."

"You try it," I said. "Show me how."

He shook his head. "All I could do is what you've been doing."

"I know what you're thinking," I said. "You don't want to show up the client. Come on. Really. I'd love to see you catch one." I handed the fly rod to him.

He shrugged, stepped up on the casting deck, and instantly showed me that he could handle a fly rod. He raked the pothole. He varied his retrieve. He changed flies.

He caught nothing, either, and after fifteen or twenty minutes he reeled up and handed the rod back to me. "Falling temperatures, low pressure system going through," he said. "Puts 'em off their feed." He climbed back to the rear of the boat, slid a spinning rod from the rack under the gunwales, and pulled a bait bucket out from under the seat. He reached into the bucket, came up with a wiggly baitfish, impaled it through the lips on a bait hook, handed the rig to Charles, and arched his eyebrows at me. "Do you mind?"

"Me?" I said. "Why should I mind?"

"I don't know," he said. "Some fly fishermen . . ."

"Not me. I'd love to see Charles catch a redfish."

Charles took my place on the casting deck and flipped his baited hook against the bank of the pothole. About one minute later his rod bowed, and two minutes after that he was holding up the first redfish I'd ever seen in person. It was a silvery, broad-shouldered, deep-chested fish built more for power than speed. Its tail glowed in subtle shades of blue and red and sported the redfish-trademark black spot.

Charles unhooked it, released it, rebaited, and a few minutes later he caught another one. After he let that one go, he said, "Guess they just don't want flies today."

I jabbed my chest with my thumb. "The old Kiss of Death." I turned to Ben. "You got another one of those spinning rods?"

He grinned. "You bet." He rigged me up and handed it to me. "Keep your line tight, and when you feel a fish, just reel up on him. Circle hook, you know."

A few minutes later I felt the tap-tap of a fish nudging my bait. I reeled up and felt the surge of a strong fish. It turned out to be a 22-inch red.

"Nice fish," said Ben. "Too bad it wasn't on the fly rod. Sorry."

"Sorry?" I said. "Hell, that was fun. I've been focused too much on fly fishing lately. Fishing with bait takes me back to my roots. Let's catch another one."

Charles and I ended up catching six or eight redfish apiece from that little pothole before the tide turned. They ate mud minnows fished right on the bottom, and they pulled hard. Some of them sported multiple spots on the bases of their tails, and I thought they were quite beautiful.

I had imagined and assumed I'd catch my first redfish sight-fishing with a fly rod from the casting deck of a flats boat with a tropical sun beating down on my shoulders. But I wasn't the least bit disappointed. Fishing was fishing, and catching was always better than not catching.

For several years, my wife and I have been spending the week before Thanksgiving visiting with family in Charleston, South Carolina. We gorge on shrimp and oysters and barbecue, prowl the streets and shops of the gorgeous old Southern city, ogle the antebellum architecture, watch the native ladies weave reed baskets, walk the beaches, take photographs, and generally enjoy a warm-weather reprieve from our frosty New Hampshire autumn. Fishing hasn't entered the equation, although it's entered my mind.

So that rainy, Thursday-morning getaway to the marsh with my local friend Charles Poindexter and our guide, Ben Floyd, was a bonus for me, a measure of the tolerance of my wife and family, and I figured I'd try to do it again when we visited next year. Maybe if I was lucky it would evolve into an annual event.

That evening we were all standing around a newspaper-covered picnic table shucking steamed oysters and drinking beer when my cell phone vibrated in my pocket. "Hey, it's Ben," he said. "You free on Saturday? I got a cancellation. S'pose to be a warm sunny day, and I owe you one. Sight-fishing weather. I know where we can find a big school of hungry reds on the bottom of the tide."

I turned to Vicki. "Am I free on Saturday?"

"Fishing, huh?" she said.

I smiled.

"You're upset you didn't get any on flies today, right?" she said.

"I'm not upset about anything. I had a great time."

"Go fishing," she said. "Unless you'd rather go to the farmers' market with us."

"I'm free," I told Ben.

Saturday was a shirtsleeve-and-sunscreen day. Ben motored out of the harbor, negotiated a labyrinth of channels and islands, then cut the motor and climbed up on his poling platform. He pointed his pole at the rim of a flat marshgrass-covered island where the falling tide had bared some mud. "There's a shelf along that edge there, water's three or four feet deep, and then it drops off into a channel. That shelf is a kind of a funnel for baitfish, and there's been a school of reds patrolling it the past few days on the falling tide. Grab a rod and climb up there and get ready."

I did as I was told. I checked the ferrules of the 8-weight, thumbnailed the point of the chartreuse Wiggler, stripped line off the reel, made a 50-foot cast, coiled the line on the deck, and pinched the fly by the bend of the hook. Locked and loaded.

I adjusted my sunglasses, tugged the brim of my hat, and felt the familiar surge of sight-fishing adrenaline zing through my veins. There's nothing like it.

Ben poled us slowly along the edge of the drop-off, both of us squinting hard at the water, and pretty soon he said, "There. Eleven o'clock. Nervous water. See the wakes?"

I saw them. It looked like three of four fish, and they were meandering along in our direction.

I got the line moving with one false cast and dropped the Wiggler about 5 feet ahead of the front wake. Perfect.

Ben laughed.

I started to ask him what was so funny. Then I saw what he was seeing. Dark shapes were zipping past us. They looked like 2-foot torpedoes. Spooked redfish. Dozens of fish. Hundreds, maybe. They left little spurts of mud in their wake. It took a couple of minutes for all of them to zoom past our boat.

"Big school," said Ben. "Your fly landed right in the middle of them. Spook one, you spook 'em all."

"Nuts," I said, or something similar.

"They'll be back," he said. "This is where they want to be. They're moving back and forth along this shelf where the food is. We'll wait."

"What I've read about redfishing," I said, "it's casting to tailing fish on the flats, like bonefish."

"We get that on the big full-moon tides, late spring and summer," Ben said. "Around here they call them tailing tides. They flood the grass flats, and the reds swarm all over them. It's a blast. Singles and pairs eating shrimp and fiddler crabs with their pretty tails waving hello. I love that. But the fall is a great time, too. They start podding up in shallow bays in September. You'll see schools of ten or fifteen fish. Around now, in November, we've got schools like this one we just spooked, fifty or a hundred fish, and by January there'll be three, four, even five hundred fish in a school. We have great sight-fishing with flies right through the winter. Cold weather in December and January puts them off their feed, but on warm, sunny days—and we have plenty of them in the winter—you'll find reds in shallow water eating shrimp and baitfish, and the only trick is not to spook them. Reds are spooky fish. Spook just one redfish in a school and they all explode."

"Like those just did," I said.

"Right. So don't shuffle your feet or make any quick moves. Don't even talk. Look down into the water, spot the fish, and don't bang your fly on their heads."

Ben eased us away from the shelf, and pretty soon we saw some fish meandering along, headed back to where they'd come from. I managed to drop my fly on the edge of the school, let it sink, twitched it a couple of times, and felt a hard tug. I tightened on him, felt his strength, lifted my rod.

Oh, yeah.

Catching redfish out of a pothole on mud minnows and spinning gear was fun. Call me a snob, but catching sighted reds on flies was way better.

We harassed that big school of redfish for about two hours before the tide bottomed out and they disappeared. We caught some, hooked others, missed several strikes. They ran from about 20 to 24 inches long—hard-pulling 5-pounders, more or less, and we spotted many larger fish (30 inches and better) in the school. We spooked them a few times and waited for them to return while the late-November Carolina sun warmed our shoulders and the scent of sea and salt and marshgrass filled our nostrils.

On the way back to the marina we stopped to play hide-and-seek with some dolphins. High overhead, bald eagles soared. We saw pelicans and herons, loons and hawks, cormorants and ducks, gulls and terns.

Everything but other fishermen. We never saw another boat until we got back to the marina.

Daisy-Chain Blues

When my father was a young man living and working in New England, he caught striped bass and weakfish (seatrout, which he called "squeteague") on his bamboo fly rod, casting from a dory into the harbors and estuaries of Massachusetts and Rhode Island.

By the time I became a young man, the stripers and weakfish were pretty much gone from New England onshore waters. For me, fly fishing was a freshwater activity. Not that I had any complaints.

I did fish the edge of the Atlantic from big oceangoing boats owned by various friends wealthier than I. We went out sometimes beyond sight of land, and we trolled spoons and plugs from rods as thick as my thumb, and we caught bluefish. Tons of bluefish, literally.

When I visited Joe Nies at his vacation place on Nantucket in the summer, we lugged his hibachi, a bag of charcoal, and a couple of surf rods out onto Cisco Beach toward evening on incoming tides. We got the coals started, then sat on the sand to wait for the schools of blues to come blitzing along. There was no sense casting blindly into the ocean, but when we saw the patch of swirling, spurting water and the panicky leaping baitfish moving down the surfline toward us, we jogged to the edge of the beach and cast plugs into the midst of the frenzy. We never had any problem catching them whenever we found them, although beaching a blue was never easy. It fought like a fish twice its size. It leaped and slogged and took off on long runs, and when you finally backed it onto the sand, its mouth would begin darting and thrashing sideways, slashing at anything it could reach, like an ankle or a thumb.

When the school got close, we could see the blues hacking and slicing away at the schools of bait. They left the water bloody. They killed wantonly. Sometimes they were so frantic that they knocked our lures into the air. Killing and eating seemed to be two different activities for bluefish.

The first fish Joe or I caught each evening got filleted and slapped instantly onto the hibachi. There has never been a fish as delicious as a 5-pound bluefish direct from the surf to the charcoal grill, still twitching.

Blues were violent, vicious, powerful fish with teeth you quickly learned to avoid. A bluefish was known as "the mouth that swims," and it never occurred to me that you could—or would want to try to—catch one on a fly rod.

It was Mike Hintlien, guiding Andy Gill and me from his boat along the Massachusetts North Shore, oh, twenty-odd years ago, who introduced me to fly-rod bluefish. By this time the striped bass had begun to return to our coastal waters, and it was the stripers that we sought. We cast shooting heads toward the surf crashing against the rocky shorelines, and I made the acquaintance of the striped bass.

But sometimes something else took my deep-running Clouser or Deceiver. "Big one," I'd grunt when I felt the pull.

Mike would know right away. "Bluefish," he'd say. Usually my line came slack a minute later. "Bit you off."

"Big blue," I'd say.

"Probably not," Mike would say. "Probably smaller than those stripers you've been catching. Stronger is all."

When the stripers were elusive, Mike would motor away from the shoreline and tell us to rig up with some wire and a big green-and-white Deceiver. He'd stop the boat in some apparently random place out of sight of land and take out a spinning outfit. It was armed with a big popper minus the hooks. Mike would cast it way the hell out there and chug it back, making it throw water, and pretty soon a patrol of bluefish would come slashing away at it. When Mike had lured the fish within casting distance, Andy and I would throw our Deceivers out amidst the frenzy, and pretty soon we'd each be tied to a bluefish.

It was pretty exciting. There was something primitive about it—about the way we went about catching them, and about the fish themselves—and you wouldn't want to do it all day. In fact, we never specifically went fly fishing for blues. Whenever we fished with Mike, we were after stripers. But for an hour or so, catching trolled-up bluefish on 8-weight fly rods sure beat casting into empty water.

It was around that time that I met Vicki. She was managing a SCUBA shop and writing for a dive magazine. She was passionate about diving, the way I was about fly fishing. I told her right off that I had no intention of ever putting my head underwater and trying to breathe, which I think disappointed her, but she was quite interested in trying fly fishing, my passion.

After a few awkward "lessons," she decided that she should learn to cast from somebody other than I. So she enrolled in a weekend class at the L. L. Bean school up in Freeport, Maine.

When she got home, she said, "Hey! I can cast." She said she'd also learned some stuff about bugs, and they'd shown her how to tie a Duncan Loop. "But you can forget that," she said. "I'm not interested in knots. Anyway, John, my teacher, he wants to take us fishing."

"Us," I said. "You mean you." Vicki was pretty cute. I could understand why a fly-fishing instructor might want to take her fishing.

"No, really," she said. "I told him about you. He said he wanted to meet you. He said he had a special place to show you. Us. So we're meeting him Tuesday morning. Okay?"

"A special place, huh? Did he indicate what kind of special?"

She shrugged. "He said something about bluefish. He said to bring an 8- or a 9-weight fly rod and some big saltwater flies. He used the word 'unique.'"

We met John at a gas station on the outskirts of Bath. An aluminum dory with a small outboard hooked on the transom was trailered behind his wagon. Vicki and I transferred our gear and piled in.

He drove through city streets and suburban neighborhoods, over country roads and, briefly, onto the interstate. I smiled. I knew what he was doing. "I wasn't planning on writing about it," I said to him.

He just smiled.

We launched John's boat somewhere in or near the estuary of the Kennebec River, and he putted among the boulders and small islands and half-exposed clam flats and patches of beach. Some of the boulders were covered with basking seals. They honked at us as we went past.

After fifteen or twenty minutes, John cut toward the jumbled rockpiles that marked the ragged shoreline, and then he slid through an opening between two house-sized boulders. The portal was narrow and tucked behind one of the tall gateway rocks. You wouldn't see it if you didn't know it was there.

We found ourselves on a round glassy pond just a few hundred yards in diameter. It felt utterly isolated. Alien, even. It was the kind of place you didn't want to spoil by talking.

John cut the motor, and we drifted over the pond on the breath of a soft breeze. Then he hissed, "There! Look."

He was standing in the stern pointing with his oar.

I tugged down the visor of my cap and looked. Then I saw it. A fish. A large grayish-green fish . . . no, wait. Two fish. No, there were more than that. Slowly swimming past our bow in single file was a long line of fish, and as my eyes adjusted, I saw that it was a full circle of fish, an endless line. A daisy chain of large bluefish circling, circling, head to tail. And they were passing about 60 feet in front of us.

I turned to Vicki. "Want to try to catch one?"

She shook her head. "I can't cast that well. Besides, those fish are scary. You do it."

I glanced at John, and he nodded.

I tried to remember what I'd read about casting to daisy-chaining tarpon. Don't bring the fly directly at the fish. Tarpon aren't used to being attacked by baitfish. Not that it should matter. These were blues. My whole experience with bluefish taught me that they'd try to kill anything that they saw.

I cast flies at those daisy-chaining blues for at least half an hour without sparking any interest whatsoever. I tried big flies and small flies, green and blue and white and red flies. I tried poppers and Clousers and Deceivers.

And then, for no apparent reason, one of them peeled off, swam up behind my little yellow Deceiver, followed it for several feet, then opened his mouth and sucked it in, just the way a striper—or a tarpon—would do.

It weighed 14 pounds, 3 ounces on John's Boga-Grip. It's still by far my biggest-ever fly-rod bluefish.

By the time we released that fish, the daisy chain had dropped out of sight. We waited and cruised around the pond, but it never reappeared.

When the tide turned later in the afternoon, a school of small stripers came into our pond, and Vicki showed me how John had taught her to cast, which was quite well indeed. She caught a bunch of schoolies on poppers, which made all three of us happy.

PART V

SOME FLIES

I want to know what I'm doing. I'd like to know the name of every insect (and tree, rock, flower, and mermaid), but I don't. Without a name, I can't look up an imitation. I can see how the natural fly is behaving, though, and pick one from a fly box that behaves likewise. If it is the right size, it will probably work. If it is also the right shape, it may work better than an imitation from a book. Design does not have to be more complicated than that.

—Datus Proper, *What the Trout Said*

Throughout these two seasons I used only one dry-fly pattern, regardless of what fly was hatching, without ever making an effort to match the hatch. Yet I think I caught as many trout as I ever did in two seasons . . .

—H. G. Tapply, *The Sportsman's Notebook*

There's alleged to be an extra satisfaction involved in catching trout on flies of one's own manufacture, but I've never noticed it. I tie my own flies because it keeps me out of mischief on long winter evenings and results in better flies than I can get from commercial sources. Also it enables me to invent all sorts of new patterns with which to confound the traditionalists and standpatters. (I doubt if the fly has ever been tied that was too freakish or fraudulent to take fish under certain conditions—and there are times when only the freak is effective. At least, I can't recall ever seeing a hatch of natural Fanwing Royal Coachmans.)

—Ed Zern, *To Hell with Fishing*

159

The Mongrel Bugger

We pushed onto the inky Bighorn from the ramp at Three Mile. A layer of pre-dawn mist ghosted over the water. The stars were just beginning to wink out, and the August sky had begun to fade from black to pewter. The PMD hatch waited a few river miles and several hours in front of us. Now it was streamer-throwin' time, and I'd won the toss.

"Black Bugger," ordered Bill from his seat at the oars.

"Mmm," I answered in what was intended to imply agreement without committing me to it.

I sat in the bow seat with my back to Bill and opened my streamer box on my knees. Bill Rohrbacher had been guiding on the Bighorn since the Crows lost their court fight, and he was on a first-name basis with every 20-inch trout that lived there. He could sniff the air and predict what was going to hatch, and how soon. I'd learned not to argue with him.

But nobody tells me what streamer to fish with.

I made my choice, tied it on, stood up, and began casting. Slap it just below that rock, lower the rod tip, strip, strip, strip. Lift, one false cast, sidearm it under the sweeper, strip, strip. Cover the water. Hit the targets. Throwin' streamers for big trout at dawn from the bow of a driftboat is mesmerizing, rhythmical, and altogether engrossing.

It's also a pretty good way to catch fish. I nailed my first trout— a standard-run 18-inch Bighorn brown—across from Snag Hole. Another whacked my streamer by the auto bodies, and by the time Bill beached the driftboat on the island below Teepee, I'd taken two more, including a rainbow that pushed 21 inches.

He leaned on his oars. "Pretty interesting," he said. "Not a single short hit. Usually you get half a dozen follows and swirls and refusals for every hookup."

"Masterful angling, obviously," I said.

"Expert guiding, more likely. Anyway, we'll see. It's my turn. Come grab these oars. Gimme your rod and let a real master have a shot."

We swapped seats. I pushed us into the currents and had begun to nose into casting distance from the bank when Bill roared, "What in hell is *this*?"

He was holding my streamer between his thumb and forefinger as if it were dangerous.

"Oh, that?" I said. "I don't know what it's called. I invented it. It's a little of this, a little of that."

"It ain't exactly a black Bugger."

"Nope. Not exactly."

"I thought I told you to tie on a black Woolly Bugger."

I shrugged.

He lowered the fly into the water and moved it back and forth. "It is similar," he mumbled. "Sort of a Muddler, too, though. A damn mongrel, that's what it is."

And that's what we decided to call it. The Mongrel Bugger.

It came out of my fly-tying vise one day-dreamy Sunday afternoon in February when the low-angled slants of the winter sun glinted off the new snow outside my window and an inch of Rebel Yell Kentucky bourbon stood in a tumbler by my elbow, and a warm summer breeze blew through my fishing-starved imagination.

I'd like to report that the Mongrel Bugger resulted from years of experimentation and refinement. I wish I'd planned it.

But on winter afternoons, I don't plan much of anything. When I sit at my fly-tying desk, I don't give a lot of thought to what I'm going to tie. I go with the Zen of it. I'm always curious to see what will happen.

On that particular February afternoon, I clamped a No. 4 streamer hook in my vise, watched a cardinal eat a sunflower seed from the birdfeeder, tied dumbbell eyes onto the front of the hook, sipped some Rebel Yell, wound back to the bend, and rummaged in my desk.

Marabou? Okay. I made a tail. It was beginning to look alarmingly like a Woolly Bugger, and damned if I was going to follow someone else's recipe.

A blue jay chased the cardinal away.

I thought about streamers. The classic landlocked salmon featherwings and bucktails I learned to tie by rote as a kid—the Warden's Worry, the Grey Ghost, the Dark Tiger, the Supervisor, the Nine-Three, the Mickey Finn. I still had drawers full of them. Relics. Never used them anymore.

Now my streamer boxes were full of Buggers and Muddlers and Clouser Deep Minnows and, most recently, Jack Gartside's elegant Soft Hackles. Suggestive, fishy, flashy, wiggly. Streamers for all occasions and all species. Nothing wrong with any of them. Each of them, in fact, featured something quite special: the Bugger's marabou tail, the Muddler's water-pushing spun-deer-hair head, the Clouser's jigging action, the Soft Hackle's undulating palmered marabou that never seems to get tangled in the bend of the hook . . .

Before I understood what was happening on that February afternoon, I had an Idea. Combine the best elements of the best flies. Mix and mingle those excellent bloodlines. It would be a mongrel. It would surely be the Perfect Streamer.

It has proved to be just that.

The Mongrel Bugger takes the marabou tail and chenille body from the Woolly Bugger. It substitutes Gartside's palmered marabou for the Bugger's wound hackle, and adds the Muddler's spun and clipped deer hair head and the Clouser's dumbbell eyes.

It's not a pattern, exactly. I think of it as a design, or a concept. In various bourbon-sipping bird-watching day-dreaming fly-tying sessions I have substituted spun wool (it sinks better) or Cactus Chenille (more flash) for the deer hair head. Eliminate the tail and chenille body and wind the marabou over the bare shank for a sparse, ethereal look in the water. Bead-chain eyes make a fly that casts easier and sinks slower. Combine different colors of marabou and palmer two feathers together for interesting mottled effects—purple and black, yellow and lime, olive and tan, orange and brown, red and white. Each might suggest a real species of fish prey: sculpin, crawfish, shiner, leech, juvenile trout.

Or maybe not. Who knows what fish think?

The Mongrel Bugger, in its various colors and sizes, has become my streamer of choice for all occasions. It took my first two (and thus far, my only) tarpons. Landlocked salmon and Chinooks. Largemouths and smallmouths. Bluefish and stripers. Pickerel and pike. Crappies and perch. Dozens and dozens of big predatory trout.

My only complaint is that whenever I tie on a Mongrel, I generally catch more fish than the people I'm fishing with, and I end up giving away handfuls of them. That's why I'm hereby going public.

Pour yourself a few fingers of Rebel Yell, gaze out your window, think fishy thoughts, and breed some Mongrels of your own.

Here's how:

1. Tie dumbbell or bead-chain eyes just behind the eye of a long-shank streamer hook. Secure with a drop of Superglue.
2. Wind back to the bend. Tie in a sprig of marabou so that it extends back about the length of the hook shank.
3. Add a few strands of Flashabou or Krystalflash on each side of the tail.
4. At the base of the tail, tie in a length of chenille, a length of gold or copper ribbing, and one or two marabou plumes by their tips.
5. Wind the thread forward to about 3/8 inch behind the lead eyes, then wind the chenille to that point and tie off.
6. Palmer the marabou forward (if you use two feathers, wind them both at the same time). Keep stroking the marabou as you wind it. The closer together you make the turns, the bulkier the fly will be. Tie off and clip the marabou butts where you tied off the chenille.
7. Counterwind the wire through the palmered marabou and tie off behind the eyes.
8. Spin one or two bunches of deer hair between the marabou and the lead eyes. Don't make the deer hair head too dense.
9. Whip-finish in front of the lead eyes.
10. Remove the fly from the vise and trim the deer hair into a bullet-shaped head, leaving a few hairs unclipped to merge with the palmered marabou.
11. Add a drop of head cement.
12. Take another sip of Rebel Yell.
13. Make another Mongrel, but don't do it exactly the same way. Remember: No two mongrels can be identical.

Bloodsuckers

$\mathbf{W}$hen I took up fly fishing in earnest, I quickly settled on the black Woolly Bugger as my all-round fly of choice. I learned that I could cast a Bugger into any stream or pond and catch whatever lived there, and even now, after I've allowed it all to become far more complicated, fly fishing can still be that simple.

Until Bob Lamm took me float-tubing on Henry's Lake in Idaho, however, it didn't occur to me to wonder what my Woolly Bugger might be actually imitating, if anything. "Leeches, in this case," Bob said as he dropped a handful of small brown Buggers into my palm. "These trout gobble leeches. The trick is to fish the fly so it acts like a leech."

I knew all about leeches. When I was a kid, we called them "bloodsuckers." Skeeter Cronin and I discovered bloodsuckers in our no-name neighborhood pond one summer afternoon nearly fifty years ago. The crappies and yellow perch had been biting so well that day that we'd run out of worms, so we shucked off our sneakers, rolled up our pantlegs, and tried to hand-capture some crayfish. After a half hour of frustration, we waded ashore to reconsider our bait problem.

That's when Skeeter pointed at my legs, crossed his eyes, grabbed his throat, stuck out his tongue, and made retching noises.

"What?" I said.

"Bloodsuckers," he gagged.

Both of us, in fact, had half a dozen black slimy leeches stuck on each leg. We yelled "Gross!" and danced around shaking our legs trying to kick them off. They were, of course, firmly attached, and when we calmed down and began to yank them off, Skeeter had an inspiration. He half-filled our empty worm can with pond water, plucked a fat leech from his ankle, and dropped it in. We watched it gyrate and squirm, then looked at each other.

In unison we whispered, "Bait!"

There are more than three hundred species of annelid worms—leeches—of which about fifty live in North American freshwater ponds and streams. They range in size from 1 to 3 inches or so, and they come in shades of black, olive, brown, orange, and maroon. Some are spotted, striped, or mottled. They are commonly called "ribbon leeches" because of their flattened bodies and their undulating swimming motion. A powerful sucker at the tail end holds them fast to their prey while they plunge the sharp proboscis at their other end into the flesh of fish, turtles, aquatic mammals, wading birds, and bare-legged boys.

Bloodsuckers are ugly, repellent creatures, especially when you discover a colony of them sucking on your legs. But fish find them irresistible. Actually, if you aren't queasy about gathering and handling them, a leech makes a terrific bait. Skeeter and I caught a lot of crappies and perch on live leeches, and we later figured out that trout and bass devoured them.

For us, though, leeches were always a last-resort bait. Handling them grossed us out, and we never could devise a faster or easier way to catch them than by standing thigh-deep in the pond until a dozen or so latched onto our bare legs.

A properly fished leech fly will catch as many fish as a live bloodsucker. Leeches move in a painfully slow, monotonous, undulating motion. The right retrieve is so slow that the fly barely moves. Point the rod tip directly at the fly, give it a 2-inch tug, and pause for the count of three. That tug straightens the marabou tail, while the pause allows the body to sink while the tail trails upward. This perfectly imitates a swimming leech.

Bob Lamm and I used slow-sinking lines that day on Henry's Lake, and we found the proper depth by casting and then counting as the line sank before beginning the retrieve. After some trial and error, I began to catch big brookies and cuttbow hybrids when I started that slow tug-pause retrieve after counting to twelve-one-thousand.

Large trout do not slash at leeches. They simply suck them in, usually when the fly is falling during the pause between tugs. I missed a lot of strikes until I learned to point the rod directly at the fly. When I focused hard on the line where it entered the water, I was usually able to detect the twitch or hesitation that meant a fish had inhaled my fly. I set the hook by pulling straight back on the line without lifting the rod. That way, if I failed to hook him, my fly remained down there where he could see it and try again.

The most productive part of a lake for fishing leech imitations is over sunken weed beds in anywhere from 6 to 20 feet of water. Leeches are most active at night and during the low-light hours— from first light to a couple hours after sunrise, and from sunset into darkness—and that's the fastest time for this kind of fishing. Any black, brown, orange, or olive Woolly Bugger will do the job, depending on the color of the resident leeches. You'll catch more fish if you "match the hatch." You can experiment with a variety of colors and sizes until the fish tell you what they're eating. Or you can wade in the water and see what gloms onto your legs.

The best leech imitations are tapered from a narrow forward end to a wider marabou tail, with a slim, fuzzy body. They should be tied on bent hooks and weighted toward the rear. You can improve any leech fly by squaring off its tail to emulate the flat ribbon shape of the rear end of a leech.

After experimenting with a variety of patterns and materials, I've concluded that my all-marabou design in suitable colors and sizes is both the easiest to tie and the best fish-fooler.

A live leech suspended under a bobber is still a deadly way to catch almost any species of freshwater fish. But a properly fished imitation works equally well—and unless you enjoy picking bloodsuckers off your bare legs, it's considerably more pleasant.

Here's how to tie an easy leech imitation:

1. Clamp a long-shank streamer hook in the vise at its middle and carefully bend it so that its front half curves upward. From the side, the hook should look like a wide V.

2. Wrap the rear half of the hook with four or five turns of lead wire.

3. Select a full marabou feather (black, brown, olive, purple, orange, red—whatever matches the leeches where you're fishing) and tie it onto the rear of the hook, forming a tail about the length of the hook shank. Do not trim the rest of the plume. For a mottled or striped effect, tie in two marabou feathers of complementary or contrasting colors (black-and-purple and orange-and-brown, for example), treating them as if each were a single feather.

4. Tie in light gold or copper wire at the base of the tail. It will add

a bit of flash and weight, create a more slender, segmented look, and secure the wound marabou.

5. Twist the remaining marabou feather around the tying thread into a "rope" and wind it forward around the hook. Tie it off and cut off the remaining marabou.

6. Counter-wind the body with the wire. Tie it off and cut off the extra wire.

7. Build a small, tapered head with the thread and whip-finish.

8. Square off the end of the tail with scissors, leaving it somewhat shorter than the fly's body. If you dampen the tail between your fingers, it's easier to work with.

9. Pick some fibers out of the marabou body with a dubbing needle to give it a shaggy appearance, then trim with scissors to taper it from its narrow, pointed head toward the wider tail end.

10. Finish with head cement.

11. Fish with confidence.

Clumped Hackles

My annual Paradise Valley pilgrimage is about a month away. Time to check my supply of Pale Morning Duns, Sulphurs, and Olives.

Over the years I have accumulated hundreds of flies to imitate these dependable spring-creek hatches. Helpful anglers have given me flies. I've salvaged other people's flies from streamside willows. I've saved the busted-off flies I've found in the lips of fish I've caught. I've even bought a few flies. And, of course, I've tied like mad before every trip.

When I open my boxes, pluck out the contents one at a time, and hold them up to the light, I realize I have a good collection of flies that I don't—and never will—use. That's why I still have them.

I don't use them because they don't work very well.

I've busted off the flies I actually use in trout mouths or streamside willows. Others have been chewed beyond usefulness. I've given quite a few away, too.

So as usual, in spite of my impressive collection, I've got to tie a new batch of flies, ones that I'll actually use.

Trout that grow up in insect factories such as the Paradise Valley spring creeks and many other fabled dry-fly rivers like the Bighorn, the Henry's Fork, and the Missouri, eat bugs all their lives. The fun of fishing these rivers is the challenge of hooking a big trout on a size-18 or -20 dry fly tied to a 6X tippet.

There are times, of course, when the fish key on nymphs or emergers. Sometimes terrestrials do the trick. I deal with those situations as I find them.

But the best part comes when they're surface-feeding selectively on mayflies.

On slick, slow-moving, gin-clear water, trout have plenty of time to make their choices. By the time they get to be 16 or 17 inches long, they've seen a million natural insects—and hundreds of fakes, too. They don't eat any old thing. To catch them, hard experience has taught me that I have to make precise, drag-free presentations with long, skinny tippets.

I've also got to show them flies that look good to eat.

There's no such thing as a never-fail pattern or design, of course, any more than there's a fly that no trout will ever try to eat. But on the spring creeks—and anywhere else that big trout sip small mayflies off smooth, slow-moving water—the imitations I have the most faith in are all tied with clumped, or bunched-up, hackles. They feature widespread tails, slender bodies of the right color that ride right on the surface film, wings located a little less than halfway back from the eye of the hook, and well-shaped thoraxes.

The key elements in imitative dry flies are: how they ride on the surface, their overall size and shape, their body color, the silhouette of their wing, and, especially, the way light plays through the wings.

Besides being a good imitation, an effective slick-water dry fly should land consistently upright, float well, endure many chomps from big, toothy brown trout, hook the fish that eat it, and not twist slender leader tippets. It should also be fairly easy to tie.

Clumped-hackle flies meet all of these criteria, and they're the ones I depend on for picky trout.

Clumping, or bunching, hackle simply involves winding a hackle feather around the shank of the hook and then shaping it with a few figure-8 turns of thread. This technique is not new, and the specific flies that I prefer are not recent inventions. My friend, the late Datus Proper, in his indispensable book *What the Trout Said*, traced the history of this design and, after many conversations with trout, made a strong case for its effectiveness.

The designs that I use on spring creeks are the Clumped-Hackle Spinner, the Clumped-Hackle Comparadun, the Clumped-Hackle No-Hackle Dun, and (with apologies to Datus) the Nearly Perfect Dun.

Here's how to tie each of them:

CLUMPED-HACKLE SPINNER

1. Wind a thread base on the shank of a standard dry-fly hook, ending at the bend of the hook.
2. Tie in a tail of six or eight stiff hackle fibers. They should be a little longer than the length of the hook. Using a dubbing needle to guide the thread, spread the tail fibers by taking a couple of tight winds underneath them.
3. Bring the thread to the halfway point on the hook shank and tie in a cream or dun hackle feather. The feather should be one size larger than you'd normally use for the hook size.
4. Bring the thread forward, make four or five turns of the hackle and tie it off.
5. Divide the hackle fibers into equal bunches on each side and figure-8 around them top and bottom to form the spinner's wings. Be careful not to make the base of the wings where they

meet the body too thin. Spinner wings are wide at the base.

6. Bring the thread back to the tail, spin dubbing onto your thread, and dub the body. Make a couple of figure 8s around the wings to build up the thorax.

7. Whip-finish a small head.

According to Datus Proper (and the trout I've encountered have told me the same thing), hackle-fiber spinner wings have better translucency than hackle tips, hair, or any synthetic material, an especially crucial consideration in spinners. In fact, clumped hackle fibers make the best wings for small- and medium-sized spinners by all the criteria.

Clumped-Hackle Comparadun

1. Tie in the tail the same as with the spinner, except make it a bit shorter.

2. Tie in a hackle feather, sized for the hook, at the halfway point of the shank, bring the thread forward, and make four or five turns of the hackle.

3. Make a couple of figure 8s around the bottom (only) of the hackle, bunching it up so that it forms a half circle over the top of the hook.

4. Dub the body and the thorax and finish the fly as you did the spinner.

The Hair-Wing Comparadun is a terrific smooth-water fly, but this clumped hackle-fiber version is easier to tie, more durable, a better floater, and has superior translucency. It also makes an excellent—and visible—spinner imitation. Substitute a wisp of brown Antron shuck for the tail and you've got a Sparkle Dun Emerger.

Clumped-Hackle No-Hackle Dun

☐ This is exactly the same fly as the Hackle-Wing Comparadun, except the hackle fibers are clumped up into a triangular, wedge-shaped wing. Looked at from straight on, the wing forms a V of about 120 degrees.

☐ This fly floats low in the water. The wedge shape that begins on the underside of the body forces it to ride upright, unlike hair- or quill-winged no-hackles, which tend to be top-heavy, tricky to balance, and prone to tipping. It's also considerably easier to tie than the other no-hackles.

NEARLY PERFECT DUN

If I were a more skillful and patient tier, I'd make Perfect Duns exactly the way Datus Proper did (he gave them their tongue-in-cheek name). He was a bit fussier with the tail than I am, and he built the fly in a slightly different sequence of steps—which, I guess, made his fly, well, perfect. Datus contended that his Perfect Dun was superior to all others by all the important fish-fooling criteria, and I agree with him. My version is awfully close.

The Perfect Dun is really a sparse Clumped-Hackle Comparadun with the addition of hackle-tip wings. So is the Nearly Perfect Dun.

1. Begin by tying in the hackle-fiber tail. Spread it and cock it up by taking two or three turns of thread under the fibers and drawing them tight against the place where the tail is tied down.

2. Bring the thread just forward of the midpoint of the shank. Tie in a matched pair of hackle tips here. The wings are the focal point of the fly and should be slightly bigger than on the natural—about the length of the hook shank. When you get them set properly, they should be slightly flared, concave sides out, and cocked slightly backwards. Datus Proper tied in hackle-tip wings by pinching them so that the stems straddled the hook shank. He figure-8'ed around them to set them in place, then bent the stems back under the shank and lashed them down before clipping off the ends. Tied on this way, the wings never pull loose or slip out of position.

3. Tie in a hackle feather in front of the wings and bring your thread behind the wings. Make just one turn of hackle in front of the wings and two turns behind them. You want a sparsely hackled fly that will not obscure the wings. The hackle suggests the mayfly's legs, supports the wings, and assures that the fly will land right. Tie off the hackle and trim away the excess.

4. Now stroke up the hackle and figure-8 under it, bunching it up so that it forms a semi-circle around the wings on the top of the fly.

5. Wind the thread back to the base of the tail and spin on dubbing to match the body color of the mayfly you want to imitate. Dub the abdomen. Keep it slender. Make a couple of figure 8s under the hackles to build up the thorax.

6. Whip-finish the head and add a drop of cement.

7. Tie it on, drift it over the fussiest trout you can find, and be prepared.

Tap's Nearenuf

For 35 years—from 1950 to 1985—my father filled two pages of *Field & Stream* with useful information for outdoorsmen. There were the 50-word "Tap's Tips"—six every month—which made Tap's name famous, and there were the 500-word "Sportsman's Notebook" articles—one per month—that needed the extra words to explain more complicated things.

I've done the math. More than 2,500 tips and 420 notebooks. That adds up to about one hundred new and useful ideas each year and over one-third of a million words—not a single one wasted—in 35 years.

What most people didn't realize, but what I, his son, understood, is that for every Tip-worthy idea that Dad selected to write about, he discarded three as impractical or wrong-headed or dumb. He field-tested everything exhaustively, and I got to go along and "help" him.

We had to do a lot of fishing and hunting to test four hundred ideas a year. Lucky me.

Sometime in the 1950s, with the trout season upon us, Dad gave teenaged me a box of dry flies. "I need your help," he said.

I opened the box. It was full of beautifully tied dry flies. My father was a perfectionist.

I started to thank him. Then I noticed that except for their sizes, which ranged from 12 to 18, every fly was identical. I arched my eyebrows at him.

"Here's the idea," he said, in pretty much the same words he used a few years later when he felt comfortable writing about it. "If I'm right, this should be the only dry fly we'll ever need. With this range of sizes, we won't have to worry about what pattern we should tie on. We'll just match the size. This way, we can concentrate on the important matter of fishing the fly properly. We've just got to figure out if I'm right."

I picked up one of the flies and held it in the palm of my hand. It had a split, wood-duck, flank-feather wing, mixed ginger-and-grizzly hackle, a stripped peacock quill body, and a pair of stripped grizzly quills, splayed wide, for tails. It reminded me a little bit of many dry-fly patterns we used, but it was identical to none of them.

"What do you call it?" I said.

He shrugged. "I don't know. It doesn't have a name. It's a mongrel. I've tried to blend the elements of our common eastern mayfly hatches—Quill Gordon, Red Quill, Hendrickson, March Brown, Gray Fox, Light Cahill, Pale Evening Dun. It doesn't really imitate any of them, as you can see. But if I'm right, we should find that it's near enough."

And that's what he eventually called it: the Nearenuf.

Several of Dad's trout-fishing friends agreed to participate in his experiment in exchange for a season's supply of Tap-tied flies, and for two full seasons of dry-fly fishing, all of us used only the Nearenuf regardless of what was hatching.

At the end of the second season, Dad insisted on candid reports from all participants. None of us felt that we'd been handicapped in the slightest or had caught fewer trout using the Nearenuf than in previous years when we'd attempted to match the hatches precisely. We spent more time stalking trout, making accurate casts, and achieving drag-free floats, and we wasted less time poking our noses into our fly boxes. As Dad wrote: "If you use the Nearenuf, your only problem will be to match the size of the hatching flies, a much simpler matter than trying first to identify whatever those things are that are dancing over the water, and then to match them in both pattern and size, which generally involves much fumble-fingered tying on and snipping off of flies the fish don't seem to want."

Dad never claimed that the Nearenuf was a magic fly. That wasn't his point. He didn't believe in magic flies. He believed that presentation was more important than imitation, and he admitted that for all he knew, an Adams or a Quill Gordon, if fished properly, would catch as many trout during any mayfly hatch as a Nearenuf.

There are many times when trout are not eating mayfly duns. On those occasions, in the experimental spirit that my father bred into me, I've found that a small pair of sharp scissors and a Nearenuf of the right size will still do the job of several boxes of flies:

- If you find trout feeding on low-riding duns in flat, slow-moving water, you can improve a Nearenuf by clipping a V-shape out of the bottom of the hackle.
- If they're eating emergers in the film, cut the bottom hackle flat and trim down the wings.
- If they're sipping spinners, clip the hackle flat on the bottom, cut off the wings, and clip a V-shape out of the top of the hackle.
- If they're gobbling nymphs in or near the surface film, cut the hackle and wings to a nub. Spit on it to make it sink.
- If they're targeting cripples, but the bottom of the hackle at an angle and amputate one wing.

With a little creative barbering, Tap's Nearenuf comes awfully close to fulfilling the promise implied by the title of the article he eventually wrote about it: "One Fly for Every Hatch."

I don't know anybody who literally fishes with just one fly. I certainly don't. Dad's point was that you would handicap yourself less than you might expect if you focused your attention on variables other than fly pattern. I think he was right.

Fly-Tying Note: If you want to substitute materials for those listed here to create a better general match for the prevalent hatches on your waters, feel free. You will not violate the principle of the Nearenuf.

TAP'S NEARENUF

1. Tie a rolled, wood-duck flank feather on top of the shank of a standard, dry-fly hook, about one-third of the way back from the eye, with the tips facing forward, so that the wing will be as tall as the shank is long. Trim the feather toward the rear of the hook, tapering it to create a smooth underbody.
2. Make a few tight turns under the wing feather to stand it up. Then split the wing and figure-8 around it. It should be cocked slightly forward with about a 45-degree angle between the two wings.
3. Bring the thread to the rear of the hook and tie in two stripped grizzly-hackle quills for a tail. The tail should be a bit longer than the length of the hook shank. Figure-8 around them to splay them out, and then fix them in place with a small drop of head cement where they meet the hook.
4. Strip the fuzz off a quill of peacock herl with a soft pencil eraser. Tie in the quill at the base of the tail, bring the thread forward to the wings, coat the thread underbody with a thin layer of head cement, and wind the peacock quill forward while the cement is still tacky. Tie off behind the wing.

5. Tie in one ginger and one grizzly-hackle feather behind the wings.
6. Wind the hackles separately, one turn behind the wing and two turns in front, and tie off behind the eye of the hook.
7. Form a neat head, whip-finish, and add a drop of head cement.

Old-Time New England Trout and Salmon Flies

Today's New England anglers enjoy a tremendous variety of options. Our cold-water streams and lakes abound with self-sustaining populations of European brown trout and western rainbows, often happily mingled with smallmouth bass and northern pike. Our warm-water ponds and lakes hold southern interlopers such as bluegills and largemouth bass. Our coastal waters teem with migratory striped bass and bluefish.

There's something for everybody, and most of us treat it like a buffet and sample everything. We've got lots of good fly fishing to choose from.

But buried deep in the marrow of most New Englanders runs a powerful strain of traditionalism. We are proud of our roots. We cherish the Good Old Days.

The Good Old New England angling days focused on brook

trout and Atlantic salmon, the only salmonids native to our waters. When the nineteenth century industrialists built dams on virtually all the running water in the six states and barricaded anadromous fish from the ocean, the salmon adapted, became landlocked, and created a unique fishery in the headwaters of what had been oceangoing rivers.

Meanwhile, native brook trout populations dwindled, but did not disappear. They remain still in northcountry lakes and rivers, and backwoods ponds and streams. They are direct descendants of the "squaretails" (as we call them) that thrived here eons before the Pilgrims landed in Plymouth.

We New Englanders value our native fish. We are stubborn and chauvinistic. We are determined to keep our traditions alive. And so we bushwhack into boggy beaver ponds and troll streamers around the rims of big Maine lakes, the way our fathers and grandfathers did.

Over the years New Englanders have created and adapted scores of fly patterns for our native brook trout and landlocked salmon. They've been around for a while, but they all still work as well as ever, and many of us prefer to use them. They do just fine on interloping fish like rainbow and brown trout, too.

Here are seven old–timers, still favorite New England trout and salmon flies among us traditionalists:

1. **Grey Ghost**: Probably the most famous of all featherwing streamers, the Grey Ghost is still Number One among those who troll flies on Sebago and Moosehead and the Rangeleys and other big lakes for landlocked salmon and squaretails. Carrie G. Stevens (who didn't use a vise) tied the world's first Grey Ghost on July 1, 1924, to imitate the smelt that were (and still are) the primary forage of salmonids in coldwater lakes. That same afternoon she tied her new creation to her leader, cast it into the Upper Dam Pool near her home on Lake Mooselookmeguntic,

and caught a 6-pound, 13-ounce brook trout. The fish won second place in the *Field & Stream* annual fishing contest and everlasting fame for Mrs. Stevens and her Grey Ghost streamer. She subsequently invented variations of the Grey Ghost that she called the Black and the Green Ghosts, and they work awfully well, too.

2. **Edson Dark Tiger:** The Dark Tiger was my father's favorite bucktail for both salmon and trout, and inevitably it became my favorite, too. Dad tied scores of Tigers every winter for us and his friends—trout-sized ones for brookies in small streams and beaver ponds, and longer ones to troll and cast for salmon, togue (lake trout), and squaretails. Dad believed the Dark Tiger was the only bucktail anyone would ever need, and it was just about the only one he ever used. It was invented by William R. Edson of Portland (Maine, of course) in 1929. The Dark Tiger featured a natural-brown bucktail wing. Edson's variation on this theme, the Light Tiger, had a wing of yellow bucktail, and works particularly well on brook trout.

3. **Ballou Special:** A. W. Ballou of Litchfield, Maine, is generally credited with being the originator of the marabou streamer, and his Special, which he created in 1921, was the first one. Ballou's original Special makes an excellent smelt imitation, which is what he intended. It quickly became a favorite of the salmon fanatics who trolled flies around the mouth of the Songo River on Sebago Lake, where the smelt gathered for their spring spawning ascent. More importantly, the Ballou Special inspired uncountable numbers of fly patterns and designs featuring marabou, not the least of which is the ever-popular Woolly Bugger and its ancestor, the Woolly Worm. Jack Gartside's Soft Hackle Streamer, which features marabou that's wound around the shank of the hook, takes the promise of Ballou's original to its ultimate incarnation.

4. **Parmacheene Belle:** Modern anglers who might sneer at brightly-colored attractor flies can comfort themselves with

the fact that this famous red-and-white wet fly was designed, perhaps whimsically, as an imitation . . . of the pectoral fin of a spawn-colored brook trout. Henry P. Wells invented the Belle in 1878 and named it after Parmacheene Lake in the Rangeley region of Maine. Whether cannibalistic brookies mistake it for one of their cousin's body parts who can say? I do know that red and white makes a deadly color combination (witness the Dardevle spoon).

5. **Cooper Bug:** Downeaster Jack Cooper invented this simple deer hair bug back in the 1930s to catch the brook trout that gobbled caddis flies off the surface of his local ponds. The fly worked so well that Cooper applied for a patent. He was denied on the grounds that his bug was too similar to Orley Tuttle's Devil Bug. Both bugs featured a sprig of deer hair bound fore and aft on top of a hook and trimmed to a head in front. Tuttle's version was bass sized; Cooper's was tied on size-12 and -14 dry-fly hooks. Sometime back in the 1950s Bob Elliot, for decades the official spokesman for Maine's angling tourism and an expert on eastern brook trout, gave a handful of Cooper's bugs to my father. Dad gave 'em a try and declared the Cooper Bug his favorite all-round searching fly. We fished them dead-drifted upstream, both to rising trout and to likely pockets. We cast them down and across and twitched 'em back. We caught a lot of brookies both ways from the streams we floated in Dad's canoe.

6. **Bivisible:** Nobody knows who was the first angler to wrap a feather around the shank of a hook and catch a trout with it. The "palmer fly" goes all the way back to the days of Charles Cotton, who made them in many colors and believed they imitated caterpillars. The Bivisible is simply a palmer fly with a turn of white hackle in front so the angler can see it easily. We New Englanders use it for probing pockets and riffles on both fast-moving, little brook-trout streams and big, brawling salmon rivers. On fast water, the Bivisible works as a generic imitation

of caddis flies, stone flies, and mayflies. It floats forever, skitters nicely, and is easy to see. You'll have to ask the trout what they're thinking when they eat it. Probably not a caterpillar.

7. **Sparrow Nymph:** Jack Gartside, the legendary Boston fly tier, cab driver, and raconteur, has been experimenting with fly-tying materials and coming up with entirely new designs and concepts for close to fifty years. Among his revolutionary inventions are the Gurgler and the Soft Hackle Streamer. The Sparrow Nymph, while nowhere near as old as the Grey Ghost, has been around for close to half a century, and it has stood the test of time. The Sparrow is the nymph equivalent of the Tap's Nearenuf. It's buggy and suggestive and works just as well twitched in a pond as it does dead-drifted in a stream. Big ones suggest stone flies; tiny ones imitate midge pupae. All the in-between sizes are, well, near enough to whatever mayfly nymphs are available.

Also by WILLIAM G. TAPPLY ...

Trout Eyes

True Tales of Adventure, Travel, and Fly-Fishing

William G. Tapply

"Bill Tapply is one of the great authentic voices of American angling—unassuming and funny, practical and wry."
—*Ted Leeson*

"Bill Tapply is one of the great authentic voices of American angling—unassuming and funny, practical and wry."

—*Ted Leeson*

"Tapply stands out for his assured prose, his good nature, and always solid angling advice."

—*Booklist*

"Bill Tapply is a profound writer who captures the essence and the fun of the fishing experience."

—Duncan Barnes, *Field & Stream*

Fly fishermen everywhere will enjoy these varied, witty, and engaging adventures by one of America's finest outdoor writers. There is a long section on trout fishing called "Brookies, Browns, and Bows," another on the challenges and excitement of saltwater fly fishing, and an exciting group of memoirs about fishing near home and in far-flung and often exotic places—like the Minipi, Bighorn, and Norfolk rivers, where the trout can beggar the imagination, and where frustration can be the occupational hazard. Trout Eyes is a love letter to the fish we pursue, the insects they eat, and the waters in which they live.

$24.95 hardcover

Also Available from SKYHORSE PUBLISHING

The Complete Book of Fly Tying
Eric Leiser

A classic from a legendary fly tyer.

$29.95 hardcover

Inventing Montana
Ted Leeson

Tales on fishing Montana's rivers and creeks.

$24.95 hardcover

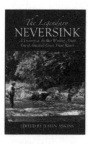

The Legendary Neversink
Edited by Justin Askins

Great writing about one of the world's best trout streams.

$29.95 hardcover

My Life Was This Big
Lefty Kreh

The autobiography of a legendary fly fisherman.

$24.95 hardcover

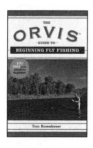

The Orvis Guide to Beginning Fly Fishing
Tom Rosenbauger

A full-color guide for anyone taking up fly fishing.

$12.95 paperback

Rivers of Restoration
Trout Unlimited's First 50 Years of Conservation
John Ross

A beautiful look at rivers and restoration.

$40.00 hardcover

Trout and Their Food
A Compact Guide for Fly Fishers
Dave Whitlock

The wisdom of a master on trout, what they eat, and how to land them.

$16.95 paperback

Redfish, Bluefish, Sheefish, Snook
Far-Flung Tales of Fly-Fishing Adventure
E. Donnall Thomas, Jr.

Join the author in Alaska, Costa Rica, the Galapagos, and more.

$24.95 hardcover